# THOMAS HARDY

by Sean Haldane

GREENWICH EXCHANGE
LONDON

**Greenwich Exchange, London**

First published in Great Britain in 2002

Printed and bound by Q3 Digital/Litho, Loughborough
Tel: 01509 213456

Typesetting and cover design by Albion Associates, London
Tel: 020 8852 4646

Greenwich Exchange Website: www.greenex.co.uk
ISBN 1-871551-33-1

To my mother,
Joan Haldane-Watkin,
thinking of St Juliot

# Contents

# Chronology

| | |
|---|---|
| **1840** | Thomas Hardy born, 2 June, at Higher Bockhampton, Dorset, eldest child of Thomas Hardy and Jemima, née Hand. |
| **1848** | Begins at Stinsford National School. Close attachment to Augusta Martin, of Kingston Maurward House, eventually broken by Jemima Hardy's intervention, and Hardy sent to Isaac Last's school in Dorchester in 1849, walking 3 miles each way. |
| **1856** | Articled to John Hicks, architect, Dorchester, until 1860, then Hicks's Assistant. Studies Latin and Greek intensively. Comes to know the poet William Barnes, head of a school next door to Hicks's office. Also becomes friendly with Horace Moule, son of Rev Henry Moule. Probably begins writing poetry, eg "Domicilium". |
| **1858?** | Attached to cousin Rebecca Sparks, Puddletown: incident after dance, forbidden by her mother to see her. |
| **1858-59** | Louisa Harding (Stinsford, Weymouth: farmer's daughter) adored from a distance. |
| **1861?** | Mary Waight, Dorchester shop assistant, seven years older, refuses Hardy's proposal of marriage. |
| **1862** | Moves to London, lives at Kilburn, becomes Assistant to Arthur Blomfield, one of the best known Victorian architects and church restorers. Visits Augusta Martin, is disillusioned. |
| **1863** | Sees much of Martha Sparks, Rebecca's sister, "in service" in Paddington area, and moves to Westbourne Park Villas, Paddington. |
| **1863 -67** | In love with, probably engaged to, Eliza Nicholls, from Kimmeredge, Dorset where her father was a coastguard, now in service in London, then living at Findon, Sussex, where her family had moved. Probably the "She" in early sonnets. He sends some poems to editors, without success, and gives up. |
| **1866? -69** | In love with Eliza's younger sister Jane Nicholls, met at Findon or possibly Dorset. "Neutral Tones" seems to mark |

end of relationship with Eliza.

**1867** Returns to Bockhampton, now a member of the Architectural Association, becomes Assistant to Hicks in Dorchester. Begins writing his first (unpublished and destroyed) novel, *The Poor Man and the Lady*. Begins relationship with the youngest Sparks sister, Tryphena, student teacher in Puddletown.

**1869-1870** Hardy in lodgings in Weymouth, working for Hicks. Jane Nicholls marries older man, Henry Beach. Hardy involved with Cassie Pole (Stinsford, possibly Weymouth. Daughter of butler at Kingston Maurward. Father said to have accused Hardy of having seduced her.)

**1870** Tryphena Sparks begins teachers' college in London. (She moves to Plymouth in 1872, marries Charles Gale 1877.)

**1870** Hardy meets Emma Lavinia Gifford, at St Juliot, Cornwall (7-11 March; 8-end of August) where he begins work on restoring church.

**1871** Publishes first novel, *Desperate Remedies*, at own expense. Further novels appear every year or two subsequently.

**1873** Moule commits suicide with razor, in rooms at Cambridge.

**1874** Hardy marries Emma, 17 September. Honeymoon in Paris, return to live in London suburbs. In subsequent years they live in at times in London, but also at Swanage, Yeovil, Sturminster Newton, and Wimbourne Minster. They have no children.

**1881** Hardy seriously ill with infection of bladder and kidneys.

**1883** Hardy and Emma move to Dorchester while a new house, "Max Gate" is built by his father and brother, to his design.

**1893** Meets Florence Henniker, with whom he conducts an emotional intrigue but who subsequently becomes simply a literary friend.

**1895** Relations with Emma become fraught with dissension, incidents of mutual ill-treatment, but more closeness survives than often thought. Hardy meets a brilliant young socialite Agnes Grove and is infatuated with her for some years.

**1896** *Jude the Obscure ("Jude the Obscene")* published and both admired and reviled. His last major novel, although *The*

| | |
|---|---|
| | *Well-Beloved* follows as a final fictional tidying up in 1897. |
| **1898** | *Wessex Poems* published, to little notice. Subsequent volumes of poetry appear every few years until his death. Hardy and Emma travel to France and Belgium together and at least temporarily revive their affection. Subsequently they contribute together to charitable organisations for "Animal Defence", and care for an army of cats. |
| **1902** | Hardy begins work on *The Dynasts.* Compared to "an ancient moulting eagle", he is tired and unwell at this time. |
| **1905** | Hardy meets Florence Dugdale, 39 years younger, and begins a secret relationship which becomes an affair, although this is obscured by the fiction, from 1910 or so, that she is as much Emma's friend as his. |
| **1910** | Accepts the Order of Merit (O.M.), but had previously refused a Knighthood (which he considered an unsuitable reward for literature). |
| **1912** | Emma dies suddenly, in November. Within a few months Florence Dugdale is living at Max Gate and (as the servants attest) sharing a bed with Hardy. However, during 1912 and 1913 Hardy writes many of the *Veteris vestigia flammae* poems to Emma, and visits St Juliot. |
| **1914** | Hardy marries Florence, 10 February. They live at Max Gate with their dog Wessex, and have no children, although Florence is worried that they might. Hardy upset by First World War, visits wounded soldiers in Dorchester hospitals making a point of visiting Germans too, and emphasising (at some risk of being accused of being unpatriotic) that they are cousins to the Saxons of Dorset. |
| **1920** | Hardy for some years is in love with Gertrude Bugler, a young married actress who is playing in a stage version of *Tess.* Florence is destructively jealous, but in spite of his obvious excitement in Gertrude's presence Hardy simply tells Gertrude to consider him her friend. |
| **1923** | The Prince of Wales (later Edward VIII) visits Max Gate and, according to Robert Graves, at one point pulls a piece of paper from his pocket and consulting it says "My mother tells me that you have written a book called… *Tess of the Durbervilles.* I must try to read it some time." Hardy cares |

less for this kind of attention than for coming to know Graves, T. E. Lawrence, Siegfried Sassoon, and Edmund Blunden, and for old friends such as Hermann Lea.

**1928** Hardy dies, after a brief decline, 11 January.

# INTRODUCTION

> You must not think me a hard-headed rationalist for all this. Half my time particularly when writing verse I "believe" ...in spectres, mysterious voices, intuitions, omens, dreams, haunted places, etc, etc.

This is Hardy writing to a philosopher acquaintance, rejecting Bergson's dualistic idea of "a line of demarcation between the inert and the living" because it leads to "an inconsistent rupture of Order." Again rejecting dualism, he wrote in a notebook that "the conception of a First Cause which the theist calls 'God', and the conception of the same that the so-styled atheist calls 'no-God', are nowadays almost exactly identical."

As a Victorian intellectual, and uneasily a self-made man sensitive to slights against his "peasant" background and needing all the means of defence available to him, Hardy was a rationalist, subscribing to Darwinism, positivism, and even (in spite of the pessimism which he described in a notebook as "the sure game... the only view of life in which you can never be disappointed") social meliorism. But in the depths of his being, which is to say as a poet, he was an animist who believed that nature is as alive as the people who move within it. In his novels an overt conflict between animism (essentially irrationalism, "peasant" superstition of the sort he had grown up with) and rationalism plays itself out. In his poems animism has full play.

Hardy agreed with the psychologist William James's point that "We live forward, we understand backward": he saw that since rationality was necessarily a retrospective summary of evidence, it could not be applied in the act of living. In another letter he attempted to resolve the rational versus irrational dilemma by defining separately *non*-rationality:

> non-rationality seems, so far as one can perceive, to be the principle of the Universe. By which I do not mean foolishness, but rather a principle for which there is no exact name, lying at the indifference-point between rationality and irrationality.

On the one side rational order, on the other, irrational disorder: most Victorians accepted this dualism, and then made a choice for order which led to much suppression of disorder in their own selves, and laid the groundwork for the late nineteenth century's most grotesque product, Freud's psychoanalysis, which in its premise that conscious order represses disorder which must then be "made conscious" through the magic of analysis perpetuated dualism for most of the 20th century. (But, as Karl Kraus said, "psychoanalysis is the disease of which it pretends to be the cure.") Toward the close of the century, however, ideas such as Jacques Monod's decisive rejection of the Bergsonian "demarcation" (between life and non life) in *Chance and Necessity* (1961), and Stephen Hawking's synthesis of order and disorder, ("God" and "non-God") in *A Brief History of Time*, brought us back to a position more close to that held courageously by Hardy, and by William James for that matter, at the century's beginning.

The courage in Hardy's rejection of dualism and his acceptance of "peasant" animism in himself and his poems (his rational acceptance of the irrational, as it were) may be less apparent from our viewpoint in the early 21st century. It caused Hardy much grief, in the form of attacks from critics for his "pessimism", and in his own conflicts as he swung, naturally, between the need for acceptance by the public which read his novels, and the need to keep the faith with the poems he described as "mood-dictated". His rational side, his Victorian "positivism", based on the influential work of Auguste Comte, led him to believe that there was no soul. Comte's label of "fetishism" for the "universal adoration of matter" had apparently stuck with Hardy: he describes Clem Yeobright, in *The Return of the Native*, more of an alter ego than most of his heroes, as suffering from this. And he helped one of his loves, Agnes Grove, with her book on snobbery *The Social Fetich* (1907), which she dedicated to him and for which he suggested the title. But although as a rationalist he might define his own aberrant thinking as fetishism, his irrationalism, his Dorset animism, led him to deny a soul to nothing, not even to buildings, stones, cliffs, and especially not to trees which are as much characters in *The Woodlanders* as the people. As he wrote in a Notebook, "I cannot help noticing countenances and tempers in objects of scenery, eg trees, hills, houses." As an old man, he let the trees block the light from a house which he had designed to receive a maximum of light, because he could not bear cutting them back and "wounding them."

The Fate of his own soul was perhaps as equivocal as his beliefs. After his last words on his death bed as officially reported, to his nurse, "Eva, what is this?", unofficially a cry to his first wife, "Em!" the disposal of his corpse was as macabre as anything in his poems or prose. He had frequently remarked, while tending his family graves at Stinsford Church, that he would be there too. But his ghoulish literary executor, the Cambridge don and archivist, Sidney Cockerell, whom as a prudent Victorian Hardy had chosen after discussion with his neurotic and depressive second wife Florence, who was intimidated by Cockerell, decided that the Nation required that the Great Man's body be deposited in Westminster Abbey. The subsequent events – Hardy's heart was cut by the obliging family doctor out of the body (which was then burnt to ashes and sent to the Abbey) and set aside for burial at Stinsford, in a biscuit tin, but first was nibbled at by one of the cats as it lay in a plate on a table – are worthy of one of Hardy's own stories, say *The Withered Hand.*

If the soul has a special affinity with the heart, as animists have tended to believe, Hardy's double nature is not spared from itself even as the dust of his heart, duly enclosed in a casket, reposes under his gravestone in Stinsford Churchyard – equidistant between the graves of his two wives. There is even, nearby, the grave (somewhat more imposing because the stone is upright, a position Hardy rejected in graves, because the stone wears down more quickly than a recumbent one) of a mid 20th century poet laureate, Cecil Day-Lewis, who saw fit to have himself parachuted, as it were, into the territory of a Great Poet he had admired and imitated. Upmarket films are now made of Hardy's novels and he has been cosily adopted by Literature. But the grotesque division of Hardy's heart from his body after death, in the name of the greater good of Literature and the Nation (Cockerell and his ilk still thought like Victorians, even a decade after the end of the First World War) can remind us that the conflict between rationalism and animism may never be resolved. What is alive, what is dead? After 87 years of life, "What is this?" If we read Hardy's poems or novels and feel at ease, we are not reading them right.

When his first bestseller (a term which came into use during his lifetime and which he loathed), *The Return of the Native*, was published he and his first wife Emma took delight in seeing people reading it on trains. Go on any train and you will still see Hardy's novels being read. It is a remarkable fact that none of his novels or poems has ever gone out of print. Yet they are not comforting. And Hardy's main academic critics and biographers twist and evade facts in order to portray him as sexually underdeveloped (Gittings) or impotent (Millgate), avaricious, pathologically depressive and gloomy, snobbish, Pooterish (after George and Weedon Grossmith's *Diary of a Nobody*), "a confirmed eavesdropper and voyeur" (Gittings): his writing still arouses indignation in comfortable people. Why does he not believe, sensibly, along with politicians and religionists, either that we live in the best of all possible worlds or that with only a little effort along approved lines, we will soon?

Supposedly impotent, Hardy had a number of sexual relationships (starting probably with an elder cousin, Rebecca Sparks: in his teens he was discovered in a compromising situation with her after a dance, and was banned from her house by her mother for some years) and two wives. He stated to a poet he trusted, Edmund Blunden, that he was sexually capable until the age of 84. Supposedly avaricious, he helped finance a distant relative, Frank George, in law studies (George was then killed in the First World War) and helped his friend Hermann Lea buy a house. Gloomy he was: he stated during the decline of his first marriage that often when he went to bed he wished he would not wake up, and he occasionally said he wished he had not been born. But he was not depressive: he cracked wicked jokes to those he knew well, fell ridiculously in love with young women, bicycled fanatically until over the age of 82, and presumably found life, on balance, worth living, since he lived it for almost 88 years. Pooterish, yes, if one takes only the evidence of his official biography, in fact an autobiography he wrote to keep his last wife happy and make her famous in her own right as its supposed author, and which is largely a tongue-in-cheek spoof of Victorian respectability. It also suited his desire to keep his rather louche private life a secret at least in prose, and in his public persona. As Siegfried Sassoon wrote after a visit: "Hardy, the Wessex wizard, wasn't there./ Good care was taken to keep him out of sight."

Hardy's real life is clear in all its passions in his poems, but he knew, realistically, that few people would read these carefully, and those few who did were precisely those who would understand what they really meant.

The Russian poet Boris Pasternak, who has some oblique affinities with Hardy, remarked that poetry in its preoccupation with life must also be preoccupied with death. Hardy, as Eliot said of Webster, "always saw the skull beneath the skin." In old age he was asked by some busybody why he did not write a poem about his and his wife's dog Wessex (beloved by Hardy in part because of his ferocious ripping of the trousers of literary visitors), and replied amiably that he would have to wait until Wessex was dead – which he did. Rationalism, and his own intellect, which was unusually powerful being for the most part self-educated, had early eliminated for him both the idea of a benevolent God and the idea of immortality. (Even on his deathbed he found the energy for a discussion of the Bible with Florence in which both agreed that there was "not a single grain of evidence that the gospel story is true.") Although a Shelleyan in his iconoclastic beliefs (more prudently hidden than those of Shelley) in free love, unlike Shelley who was a complete Platonist although an atheist (an *idealistic* rationalist, as so many of the Victorians who followed him were although Shelley in his poems, at least, knew about the suppurating inner "Fiend" that such idealism engendered), Hardy could not believe that there was anything much which either transcended or lay behind physical reality. Shelley wrote idealistically in his Preface to *The Revolt of Islam* that "The erroneous and degrading idea which men have conceived of a Supreme Being, for instance, is spoken against but not the Supreme Being itself." Hardy dared in novels and poems to speak against, or question the Supreme Being: though more cautious than Shelley, he was more courageous. Mary Shelley wrote in her note on *Prometheus Unbound* that "Shelley believed that mankind had only to will that there would be no evil and there would be none." Hardy could never have believed this. Characteristically, a poem he wrote in Italy on Shelley's Skylark (the one Shelley had addressed: "Hail to thee blithe spirit! Bird thou never wert!") described the actual skylark's body," a pinch of unseen, unguarded dust."

Hardy never permitted himself to hope for the best, and those of his fictional characters who do are usually defeated. But his instinctive animism, irrational or not, saved him from cynicism. His poems and novels contain passages of extraordinary beauty which, although seldom not at the same time sad with mortality, do provide some hope for life in itself. Like the later Italian poet Eugenio Montale, Hardy rejected any philosophy of vitalism – of life for life's sake, what Montale called "brute vitalism" – but believed that the dead survived, bleakly to be sure, in the memory of others. Montale (who had read some Hardy) wrote a poem after the death of his wife "Mosca" about how her brother who had died mad and was swiftly forgotten by the world after having failed as a composer of music now only existed in Montale's brain. Hardy wrote several poems on this kind of theme, for example "His Immortality" which ends:

> Lastly I ask now old and chill
> If aught of him remain unperished still;
> And find, in me alone, a feeble spark,
> Dying amid the dark.

For Hardy, like earlier English poets, death was the Leveller. "Voices from Things Growing in a Country Churchyard", written at the age of 81, begins with a reference to a girl he had been infatuated with at the age of about 10:

> These flowers are I, poor Fanny Hurd,
> Sir or Madam,
> A litttle girl here sepultured.
> Once I flit-fluttered like a bird
> Above the grass, as now I wave
> In daisy shapes above my grave,
> All day cheerily,
> All night eerily!

Another girl he was in love with at a distance, in his teens, Louisa Harding, appears in "Transformations" becoming a rose:

> These grasses must be made
> Of her who often prayed,
> Last century, for repose;
> And the fair girl long ago
> Whom I often tried to know
> May be entering this rose.

This book has no particular thesis about Hardy's poetry: that it is poetry is enough, and poetry has too peculiar a relation to time to be summed up in a thesis which inevitably imposes historical context. With regard to Hardy's prose fiction, this book does, however, state a thesis of sorts: that Hardy was the last great *literary* novelist and thus possibly the last great novelist in English, as well as being the greatest poetic novelist.

Hardy completed his novels just as film arrived on the scene: the beginning of film is usually taken as 1896, the year of publication of his last novel, *Jude the Obscure,* which still fully carries the literary burden of having to provide the descriptions of scenes and background which in the early 1900s began to be gradually abandoned. Paradoxically, in his verse drama, *The Dynasts*, written in the early 1900s, Hardy himself uses a technique of swooping over a vast panorama of events, which anticipates the cinematic: it can be compared to the technique in the early films of Sergei Eisenstein, although its origin seems to be (as Susan Dean has argued) in the pre-film technology of the late Victorian "diorama".

Subsequent novelists have all been influenced by film, whether willingly or not. The detailed description of scenes and people has dropped out: it cannot compete with the movie screen. Modern novels even seem to move, like a film, from frame to frame, and dialogue often reads like a film script. That some reactionary novelists (masquerading as progressives) such as James Joyce and Samuel Becket beat a retreat inwards, away from the prospect of failure in competition with the movies in depicting outside reality, to stream-of-consciousness, simply proves the point: no novel of the 20th century is uninfluenced by film, and therefore no novel can be described as wholly part of the literary tradition in which, after all, the novel has its origin. There have of course been various rearguard actions – struggles to preserve the traditional novel through brilliantly self-conscious or "postmodernist" manipulations of the genre as for example the "magic realism" of Garcia Marques. And occasionally a poet will feel compelled to write a novel, in which poetry inevitably breathes. An example is Pasternak. Although *Dr Zhivago* is more overtly political than anything in Hardy, it is like Hardy's novels in its "impossible" coincidences and its pervasive animism ("cabbages, blue and wrinkled with cold", a snowstorm seen as a raging beast). But it has made a more convincing film than any of Hardy's novels because it is already film-like: huge chunks of the characters' experience are allowed to fall out of the narrative which consists of vivid, unlinked scenes. The script even of a long film is only 30 or 40 pages long. Language is only a minor part of "the pictures."

Perhaps the most relevant point to the understanding of Hardy, in comparing his novels to their film versions where these exist, is that this reveals the place of poetry in Hardy's prose. Many novels, before and after Hardy's (and one or two of Hardy's own, among his "novels of ingenuity") contain no poetry. Like film: if it has any affinity to another form of expression it is not to poetry but to visual art, as a form of moving painting. Poetry is still something of a mystery. (Neuroscientists, for example, have no way of explaining the genesis of a poem, its "inspiration".) It may ultimately resist definition. But the facts that most of Hardy's novels can be described as in some sense "poetic" and that many of his apparent poems can be described as "prosaic" may at least provoke interesting questions about the distinctions between poetry and prose.

But here again we arrive at Hardy's duality: he was a great and swiftly famous novelist who was not taken seriously for most of his lifetime as a poet but he supposedly gave up novels and turned back to poetry (a fiction:

he had in fact never left it) because he took it much more seriously (in spite of his faking it at times) than his prose. Similarly with his view of existence: he was officially a rationalist, but unofficially an animist. It was not his rationalism, or Victorian high mindedness, which brought the Victorian critic Edmund Gosse to accuse him of emerging from Wessex (a region, now a commonplace in everything from transport to schools and water boards, which only existed in history books until Hardy re-animated it in his work) to shake his fist at God.

Ironically, in his anger at the Victorian Father God, Hardy became, unwittingly, a kind of God in his own right. He states, famously, at the end of *Tess of the Durbervilles*, in a quotation from the Greek tragedian Aeschylus, that "the President of the Immortals had… ended his sport with Tess." But then, who had invented Tess in the first place? Not Zeus but Hardy himself. The "fate" in his novels, the tragic workings of character as destiny, the deterministic nature of the novels' vision of a Monod-like chance and necessity, relieved only on a very small and local scale by the occasional, almost chance exercise of a human will, are all Hardy's "creations": he is after all a novelist, and if as nowadays the scriptwriter or producer of the most trivial TV programme or film are allowed to rush, as they do, to claim the title of "creator", then he can claim it for his novels especially in so far as they (essentially unlike poems) are willed into being.

This is another reason for emphasising the unwilled, mysterious quality of poetry which is intrinsic to Hardy's novels and perhaps to all novels that endure. They are not poems, but most of them contain poetry. (The exceptions are precisely those puzzle novels in which an intricate plot is carried through predetermined steps to a wholly planned conclusion.) In practical terms, all this may mean is that once he started writing his "novels of character and circumstance" he became carried away by the circumstance he allowed them to contain – which of course was a concentration of elements from circumstances and events in his own memory – and he lost control. To the extent that by the end of *Tess of the Durbervilles* he was as moved and upset as any potential reader by her Fate.

This Fate often annoys readers: Hardy is playing God indeed, if Tess's future is determined by such "chance" events as a letter being slipped under a door and, by accident, under a carpet where it lies hidden. It can be argued that she was careless in not double-checking that the letter had slid in well, and that when she had discovered her error and did not correct it, the weakness of her character came into play. But Hardy knows this: it is one of his novels of character and circumstance. His Godlike manipulation of circumstance in his novels may even be a compensation for his helpless knowledge as a poet that circumstance is quite out of his control. But this tendency for seemingly unrealistic coincidence to turn up in novels by a poet is not unique. Pasternak, for example, was much criticised for the coincidences in *Dr Zhivago*. Perhaps it is simply consistent with a poet's experience, and not a manipulation at all. Perhaps the last laugh about "chance and necessity" will be, after all, with the poets. Hardy studied Moivre's *Doctrines of Chance*, the favourite book of the villain Dare in *A Laodicean*. The unfairly discredited Viennese biologist Paul Kammerer had more to say about the subject in his (untranslated) *Das Gesetz der Serie* (The Law of Series).

Hardy would rationalise this capacity to be carried away by his inspiration as "an ecstatic temperament" which he said he had since boyhood, and which he implied, characteristically, was morbid. Luckily, he had not read widely enough in anthropology (then an infant science) to identify his own irrationalism, although he acknowledged it in the quotation given at the head of this Introduction, as the actual reverse of positivism: animism, in which everything is alive. If he had recognised this he might have tried successfully to reason it away. After all, he did not necessarily enjoy the suffering it brought him (and his first wife Emma, with whom he empathised with all animal life to the extent that his drawing room became almost uninhabitable because of the planks they had set out between armchairs and sofas for their cats to be able to cross easily to and fro), especially as in late middle age he found that

> ...Time, to make me grieve,
> Part steals, lets part abide;
> And shakes this fragile frame at eve
> With throbbings of noontide.

Hardy's current reputation can be gauged by the continuing appearance of studies about him on the academic production line, the fact that his poems and novels have never gone out of print, the appearance every so often of films based on his novels, and the increasing acceptance that he is not just a major English novelist but one of England's greatest poets.

# 1 Life

In old age, in one of his visits to Stinsford churchyard, Hardy saw the ghost of his grandfather, a man wearing a green jacket, and passed the time of day with him. If he occasionally walks in Stinsford now, he is likely to become lost. The A35 dual carriageway splits the churchyard off from the village of Stinsford and the house he last lived in on the outskirts of Dorchester (where there is now a Thomas Hardy shopping centre). The nearby big house at Kingston Maurward where as a boy he thrilled to the silken "frou frou" of the dress of its chatelaine Augusta Martin, is now an Agricultural College. The house he was born in, two miles away at Bockhampton, past odiferous chicken farms with corrugated iron outbuildings, is surrounded by woods (some of them plantations) in which, with the distant roar of the dual carriageway in the background, visitors can walk along American style "Nature Trails."

It is worth, though, making some imaginative effort to recreate the place into which Hardy was born, on 2 June 1840 – under the dualistic sign of Gemini – since it contained the main elements of the Wessex he was to invent. The cottage with the thatched roof, carefully preserved, is more or less the same. So are the original, mixed woods of oak, ash, holly, bluebells in May, thrushes and warblers singing. The notice board by the Nature Trails gives a chalked in list of whatever songs are currently in the programme. But down toward the chicken farms were other thatched tenant cottages, subsequently pulled down, with orchards of plum, apple and cherry, and fields with dairy cows. And up behind the cottage, where the plantations are now, was an extension of the great heathland – head-high bracken, impenetrable furze, boggy puddles – which used to cover much of Dorset and which Hardy made famous in his novels as Egdon Heath.

The cottage was, then, at the conjunction of three landscapes, as described in a poem "Domicilium" written in Hardy's late teens. Woods:

> High beeches, bending, hang a veil of boughs,
> And sweep against the roof.

Domesticated gardens and fields:

> ... such hardy flowers
> As flourish best untrained... And further still
> A field; then cottages with trees, and last
> The distant hills and sky.

And the heath:

> Behind, the scene is wilder. Heath and furze
> Are everything that seems to grow and thrive
> Upon the uneven ground.

The three landscapes were to become the essentials of Hardy's Wessex: woods (*Under the Greenwood Tree, The Woodlanders*), fields (*Tess of the Durbervilles, Far From the Madding Crowd*) and heath (*The Return of the Native*). Three miles away, on the other side of Stinsford, was the county town of Dorchester (*The Mayor of Casterbridge*). Eight miles to the Southwest was the English Channel, at Weymouth (*The Trumpet Major, The Well-Beloved).*

He was put into a basket at birth since the doctor, assuming he was dead, turned his attentions to his mother. But he stirred, and the midwife called out: "Dead! Stop a minute: he's alive enough, sure!" The stories of how he grew up physically feeble and small, but intellectually and emotionally precocious, how he was discovered one day in his cradle with a snake that had crept in to sleep with him, how he learned the violin early and used to play it at dances until he almost dropped, how he sat amid the head-high ferns at the edge of the heath and decided he was not sure whether he wanted to grow up, are given by himself directly in his autobiography (known spuriously as *The Life of Thomas Hardy*, by his wife Florence Hardy) and indirectly in poems, and in the standard biographies by Millgate and Seymour-Smith. The main chronological events are summarised at the beginning of this book. This chapter, given the impossibility of summarising Hardy's 87 years convincingly, will single out several events which are crucial to his novels and his poems.

First it is worth noting Hardy's own emphasis on his "ecstatic temperament" in childhood. He relates this to his being moved to tears by music, and to a ritual in which he would wait for the shining of the evening sun with a "chromatic effect" into a red-painted staircase, and sing the hymn "And now another day is gone". His choice of words in his few prose descriptions of himself was always careful, and he knew his Greek:

"ecstatic" is from "ekstasos" – standing or being outside the self. But in the examples he gives, he is not describing a supernatural detachment from reality, but a sort of reverie in which he is both inside and outside himself, and very much inside the outside world – of music, setting sunlight, of the ferns behind the cottage or, to take an example from *Jude the Obscure*, the identification with light passing through the lattices of a straw hat held in front of the eyes. Hardy had a strong temperamental affinity with the poet whose ideas of poetry would influence him most, Shelley, although his actual way of living and writing was not in the least like Shelley's. In an essay "On Life" which Hardy would not have read (it existed only in manuscript during his life), Shelley wrote,

> Those who are subject to the state called reverie feel as if their nature were dissolved into the surrounding universe, or as if the surrounding universe were absorbed into their being. They are conscious of no distinction. And these are states which precede, or accompany, or follow an unusually intense and vivid apprehension of life. As men grow up this power commonly decays, and they become mechanical and habitual agents.

To avoid this common fate, Shelley became an exile, a poetic revolutionary, a rocket that fizzled across the sky before plunging prematurely into the sea. Hardy avoided it more shrewdly, by cultivating a double life. The Pooter side of Hardy was not simply a front: he seriously knew that (unlike the privileged Shelley) if he did not claw himself up from his country background he would stay disintegrating in the mud, a mere freak, like his cousin John Antell, a drunken, angry shoemaker who had studied Latin once, a sort of Jude. Hardy never mentioned, but would have known about, the early 19th century poet John Clare who, though not helped by a childhood fall from a hay-wagon which seems to have caused epilepsy and eventual psychosis, did disintegrate. The only saving choice for Hardy was to become a self made man – as in his own way his closest poetic friend William Barnes did as a school teacher, then Cambridge educated parson, though he remained rooted in Dorset.

So from an early age Hardy seems to have been something of a "little old man" (a less menacing version of the emotionally crippled Father Time in *Jude the Obscure*), often reading from Latin and Greek as he walked along the country lanes 3 miles each way every day to school in Dorchester, then later to his apprenticeship in an architect's office.

Nevertheless there was one emotional drama in his childhood: the power struggle between his mother, Jemima Hardy (née Hand: they were, like Clem and Mrs Yeobright in *The Return of the Native*, "as close as two hands") and the lady of the manor, Mrs Augusta Martin of Kingston Maurward, who was infatuated with Hardy when he was 9 and 10 years old. Presumably she could see something in this sober little boy that others could not. Perhaps it was simply that he was in love with her: he spent much time on her knees being cuddled to her bosom, and kissed on the lips, and since what is known about any unorthodox sexual relationship is almost always insufficient to the facts, it is likely that she would have taken him for a cuddle when she had her afternoon naps as well. The formidable Jemima stepped in and confronted Mrs Martin, and broke the relationship by sending Hardy into Dorchester to a non-conformist school instead of the Stinsford parish school of which Mrs Martin was patron. The "frou frou" of her silk dress haunted him for years, and when he came to London (where she had moved) as a young man, he wasted no time in paying her a visit, undoubtedly with the hope of at last consummating their relationship, and undeterred in his mind that she was then approaching 60 though he balked at the reality which confronted him. This relationship may be responsible for many scenes in his novels, most notably the extraordinary vividness of his descriptions in *Desperate Remedies* of how Cytherea is clasped in bed by her employer, the older Cytherea. These scenes, it has been speculated, originate from Lesbian experiences of his girl cousins "in service" to lonely mistresses, but they are more likely displacements of Hardy's own experiences. Certainly, the relation with Augusta Martin breached any taboo about sexual love across wide age differences: Pierston and his three Avices in *The Well Beloved*, Swithin and Viviette in *Two on a Tower*, Fitzpiers and Felice Charmond in *The Woodlanders* may be incompatible, but not because of the age difference. And after all, Hardy did not think twice of marrying the 34 year old Florence Dugdale when he was 73.

## The hanged woman

In his autobiography (the *Life* he wrote under Florence Hardy's name), Hardy mentions the incident, in the year he turned 16, of recalling just before breakfast that a man was due to be hanged at Dorchester gaol, and hurrying out with the family telescope to a high spot on the heath from where he could watch the execution, almost three miles away.

At the moment of his placing the glass to his eye the white figure dropped downwards, and the faint note of the town clock struck eight.

> The whole thing had been so sudden that the glass nearly fell from Hardy's hands. He seemed alone on the heath with the hanged man, and crept homeward wishing he had not been so curious. It was the second and last execution he witnessed, the first having been that of a woman, two or three years earlier, when he stood close to the gallows.

The first execution is described in a letter Hardy wrote in 1926, at the age of 85, to an acquaintance, Lady Pinney. He had asked her, "Can you find out about Martha Brown? She lived over there... I saw her hanged when I was sixteen."

Lady Pinney subsequently wrote to Hardy about the murder, which was motivated by the husband's unfaithfulness. (Hardy would have known this, at the time of execution.) He replied:

> My sincere thanks for the details... about that unhappy woman Martha Brown, whom I am ashamed to say I saw hanged, my only excuse being that I was but a youth, and had to be in town at that time for other reasons... I remember what a fine figure she showed against the sky as she hung in the misty rain, and how the tight black silk gown set off her shape as she wheeled half-round and back.

As Martin Seymour-Smith points out,

> His reaction has the expected sexual component, although his account is unusual in not troubling to disguise it. There is nothing "unconscious" about the effect on him of the shape of a woman's body: one of the important things about Hardy is that he did not shirk "unpleasant facts".

However, he may have blurred the chronology ("when I was sixteen" and "two or three years earlier" [than sixteen] not being compatible) or conflated the two hangings in his memory as an old man. His reaction to both hangings was shame at his own excitement. Both are seen as part of a wider scene – from three miles away through a telescope, and a crowd.

The hanging of Martha Brown must have etched in his mind a powerful association of women's sexuality, her potential murderousness, and the retribution exacted on her by men. The link with *Tess*, perhaps his greatest novel to come, is evident. But it is not necessary to be Freudian about this pre-Freudian experience. Or contemporary: that some people hang themselves for sexual pleasure is now a newspaper cliché. Hardy provides no evidence in his work or letters of an interest in the sensation of being hanged. Rather, the image of desire as the rain caused the silk gown to stick to her body as it perhaps trembled or shuddered in death as in an orgasm – being punished for an act of passion. Perhaps he was even younger than sixteen, and close to the memory of Augusta Martin's excitement as she held the little Tommy on her lap – for which she and he were punished by separation enforced by the morally outraged Jemima. This is speculation. But it is clear from the evidence of his poems and novels that one or more events in Hardy's childhood or adolescence must have enabled him to break through the Victorian taboos about thinking of women as sexual, passionate beings. The hanging of Martha Brown may have been one of these events. Although his shame at having witnessed it, and having desired her corpse as "she wheeled half-round and back" may have contributed to a certain sexual furtiveness which marred his later life, it also may have opened up an awareness of what Rilke was to call beauty as "the first apprehension of the terrible". By the time he was 85, at least, Hardy was able, as Seymour-Smith points out, to face his feelings without shame. But this was a long life of the unconscious becoming conscious through his novels and poems.

## Horace Moule

Much has been made by biographers of Hardy's friendship with Horace Moule (1832-1873), son of a Dorchester clergyman renowned for good works, who was brilliant, scholarly, and obscurely troubled. Eventually, he killed himself, in his lodgings at Cambridge, by cutting his throat with a razor. He had been suffering from doubts in his faith, had failed in a teaching job at Marlborough, had been drinking himself to death for years, and it is thought that a respectable governess to whom he had become engaged had broken the engagement. He may also have been tormented by guilt at having fathered an illegitimate child on a Dorset girl. This event is only recorded in a statement by Hardy's widow Florence to R.L. Purdy that Hardy had told her that, in Millgate's words, "Moule had had an affair with a "Mixen Lane" girl of doubtful reputation who became pregnant and was shipped off to Australia where her son – of whom Moule might or might not have been the father – was later hanged."

Much transmuted, aspects of Moule seem to appear in many of Hardy's novels ranging from the character of Knight in *A Pair of Blue Eyes*, through Angel Clare and his family in *Tess of the Durbervilles*, to the dripping of the villain (but also preacher) Alec Durberville's blood through the ceiling of the room below after Tess has plunged a knife into his chest.

Under the baneful influence of Freud (whose crush on Wilhelm Fliess has been projected, it seems, onto the entire 20th century), it has of course been claimed that Hardy's relationship with Moule was homosexual. That Hardy "loved" Moule in a way that, before Freud, was permitted between male friends without implications of genital contact or the wish for it, is beyond question. Moule was certainly Hardy's mentor in some things (not in poetry or novel-writing, about which he knew nothing), but not a "tutor" in the Shakespearean sense, of a pederast. His hushed up secret life was his misbehaviour with women.

Moule occasionally appears in Hardy's poems as "my friend." The poem, "Standing by the Mantelpiece (H. M. M. 1873)" refers to Moule in the year of his death. That it only appeared posthumously in *Winter Words* has provided fuel for an assumption by Millgate of a supposedly homosexual subtext. It is in the form of a discourse by a speaker who is standing by the mantelpiece where there is a candle:

> This candle-wax is shaping to a shroud
> To-night. (They call it that, as you may know) –
> By touching it the claimant is avowed,
> And hence I press it with my finger so.
>
> Tonight. To me twice night, that should have been
> The radiance of the midmost tick of noon,
> And close around me wintertime is seen
> That might have shone the veriest day of June!
>
> But since all's lost, and nothing really lies
> Above but shade, and shadier shade below,
> Let me make clear, before one of us dies,
> My mind to yours, just now embittered so...

The further three stanzas continue in the same vein and end with the narrator pressing his "finger so". (The "shroud" is a traditional term for the shape of the melting wax on a candle, like a funeral sheet.) Whatever the reader makes of this poem, it must be remembered that since it was published late it may also have been written late. The academic disputes about who is speaking to whom (Moule to his wronged girlfriend? She to him? Moule to Hardy? Hardy to Moule? Moule to his brother Charles who was in the room next door when he cut his throat?) neglect the possibility that at one level of the poem this is Hardy, as an old man, speaking his mind at last: *he* "claims its drape", ie is ready to die, as his best friend did – almost to *will* himself to die, as Moule did in killing himself. His wish to die, having had enough, to snuff life's candle (to "snuff it", vulgarly) – brings Moule to mind, along with a situation from 1873 which is not clear. That it was homosexual seems far-fetched, from what is known of both men. That it was sexual, in part, seems clear from the imagery of the melting candle which is, yes, phallic.

Was there perhaps something between Moule's mysterious wronged girl, and Hardy? Something that echoes through *A Girl with Blue Eyes*, which though it incorporates Emma (who never knew Moule) portrays the rivalry over a girl between two male friends who resemble partly Moule and Hardy? (Though Knight's priggishness does not seem at all like Moule, his intellectual make-up may reflect the side of Moule that could not live with his cruder self). It seems that the speaker is not only ready to snuff out his life, he is snuffing it out in its sexual aspect, renouncing something. To put it bluntly, this something is less likely to be buggery than a sexual relationship (a use of the penis/candle) with a woman.

*Tess of the Durbervilles* may contain some clues about the Moule story. Tess is a country girl who is destroyed by two men: Angel, a high-minded free-thinking but Christian son of a good clergyman, and Alex, a villain who nevertheless becomes an itinerant preacher. It is not far-fetched to see these two "As" as two sides of the same person, and each may contain something of Moule. Which suggests that the original of Tess (assuming there was one as Hardy family traditions maintained) may have been Moule's abandoned Dorset girl who is probably (as Gittings points out) described in "She at his Funeral" (dated elusively by Hardy 187-, but almost certainly 1873, the year of Moule's death):

> They bear him to his resting place
> In slow procession sweeping by;
> I follow at a stranger's space;
> His kindred they, his sweetheart I.
> Unchanged my gown of garish dye,
> Though sable sad is their attire;

But they stand around with griefless eye,
Whilst my regret consumes like fire!

Gittings claims that the "She" of Hardy's early sonnets ("She to Him", etc.) is a certain "H. A.", mentioned in Hardy's letters from London to his sister Mary, but Millgate claims that H. A. was Henrietta Adams, a middle aged friend of Hardy's mother's. It is, as Millgate shows, most likely that the "She" of the sonnets is Eliza Nicholls, a religious young lady to whom Hardy was engaged between about 1863 and 1867 and who, still unmarried, arrived to claim him in 1913, shortly after Emma's death: he told her he was about to marry Florence. Eliza can hardly be the same "She" as "She at his Funeral." But this She with her "gown of garish dye" is even reminiscent of the "Ruined Maid" of an outwardly humorous poem, dated 1866:

"O 'MELIA, my dear, this does everything crown!
Who could have supposed I should meet you in Town?
And whence such fair garments, such prosperi-ty?" –
"O didn't you know I'd been ruined?" said she.

– "You left us in tatters, without shoes or socks,
Tired of digging potatoes, and spudding up docks
And now you've gay bracelets and bright feathers three!"
"Yes: that's how we dress when we're ruined," said she...

Gittings suggests (a red herring if Millgate is right) that H. A. may be the woman described in "The Mound", which appeared in Hardy's posthumous volume, apparently having been kept back for many years.

Just for a moment pause:-
Just here it was;
And here through the thin thorn hedge, by the rays of the moon,
I can see the tree in the field, and beside it the mound
Now sheeted with snow whereon we sat that June
When it was green and round,
And she crazed my mind by what she coolly told –
The history of her undoing,
(As I saw it) but she called "comradeship,"
That bred in her no rueing:
And saying she'd not be bound
For life to one man, young, ripe-yeared, or old,

Left me – an innocent simpleton to her viewing;
For, though my accompt of years outscored her own,
        Hers had more hotly flown…
We never met again by this green mound,
To press as once so often lip on lip,
        And palter, and pause:
        Yes; here it was !

"Crazed my mind" is strong stuff for Hardy. And in earlier drafts of the poem "hotly" was "feverishly" and "fervidly". If this independent-minded woman was the same girl impregnated by Moule, this might explain the poet's shock – a double one – in "The Mound", as well as the emotion of "Standing by the Mantlepiece". A very late poem, written 1927, "An Experience", although it has been taken by Seymour-Smith to refer to Hardy's memory, as an old man, of Moule, may in fact refer to an experience closer to the time of Moule's death: as in "The Mound", the word "crazed" occurs: "What I, though cobwebbed, crazed / Was never to forget, / My friend, / Was never to forget."

## Hardy's early loves

Hardy's early love affairs are tangled, and of course obscured. Each bio–grapher seems to pursue a different line and have a favourite among possible candidates for the women addressed in Hardy's early love poems – none completely without evidence, although all serious biographers agree that the thesis of Lois Deacon in *Providence and Mr Hardy*, that Hardy fathered an illegitimate child on his cousin Tryphena Sparks is totally without evidence. Gittings, on the other hand, is a protagonist of Tryphena as Hardy's main love. And indeed there is some evidence that Hardy followed his early passion for Rebecca Sparks with a passion for her younger sister Martha, then another passion for the youngest sister Tryphena, who eventually married another man. Millgate discovered the evidence (not apparently known to Gittings) that Hardy was in love with Eliza Nicholls, and that this relationship foundered when Hardy fell in love with her more sophisticated and "fast" younger sister Jane, who abandoned him and married another man in 1869. To muddle matters still further there is another name linked with Hardy in the late 1860s, another maidservant, in Dorset, named Cassie Pole, said to be a daughter of the former butler at Kingston Maurward, who accused him of seducing her – but nothing more of this incident is known.

Seymour-Smith balances Millgate's evidence for Eliza and Jane Nicholls against Gittings's evidence for Tryphena, and favours Millgate's. This is convincing enough. (And a point not mentioned so far in biographies is that the heroine of *The Mayor of Casterbridge*, whose hero is Michael Henchard, is called Elizabeth Jane – a neat conflation of the Nicholls girls.) But of course *all* these relationships may have occurred. And if so, which of them, if any, might have been with the woman who appears in "An Experience" and "The Mound"? If this woman is in fact the one impregnated and cast off by Moule, a disturbing possibility emerges which may enlighten some of the mysteries of Hardy's biography: that he and Moule had a love affair with the same woman.

First, though, the chronology is confused. It is assumed by Millgate and therefore others that the "lurid tale" of the girl from "Mixen Lane" (a haunt of prostitutes in the Fordington area of Dorchester where Moule's father was vicar) dates from "the late 1850s or early 1860s when Moule was living at Fordington", but Millgate goes on to admit that she is probably the woman who is "a distant observer" in "She at His Funeral", dated 1873 – which does not square with the notion of an immediate emigration to Australia after an affair in 1860 or so.

Hardy's version to Florence is almost guaranteed to be elusive, and via Purdy it is third hand. Perhaps "Mixen Lane" was only an allusion to the woman having been of a disreputable background – or it may have been one of Hardy's typical decoys. It is of interest that he felt the need to mention her to Florence at all, particularly if there was some doubt of Moule's being the father of the woman's son. The obvious connection was noted by Gittings, and is generally accepted, that this supposed son of Moule's may contribute to the origin of little Father Time in *Jude the Obscure* – Jude's son by the sluttish Arabella, who is brought to Australia, then back to England where he is taken in by Jude and Sue and eventually hangs himself and their children "because we are too menny". But might he have been Hardy's son? Or might Hardy (and Moule) not have been sure? And again, who was his mother?

The summer of 1869, mainly at Weymouth where Hardy was working as an architect, may have concentrated three relationships at once. There may have been the end of the relationship with Jane Nicholls, when she married in July: several poems placed "Weymouth" suggest this marriage was a sudden retreat, approved by her father, from a serious affair with

Hardy. If she is the woman who figures in "The Place on the Map", which seems likely (see below), there is also the conjecture of a possible pregnancy in which either Hardy or the prospective husband may have been the father. Then there is the presence of Tryphena who may have been, in spite of all the conjecture (by Gittings, and most irresponsibly by Lois Deacon who invents a child between Hardy and Tryphena, fathered when by all accounts he was engaged to Emma Gifford) simply a close friend: this fits the tone of Hardy's poem "Thoughts of Phena", 1890. And there was the liaison with Cassie Pole. Given the logistics of what we know of Hardy's life, if there was in fact a woman who might have been impregnated by either Hardy or Moule (who visited the Dorchester area frequently) Cassie Pole may be the only one who would fit into the picture. But of course this is conjecture, and it is easy to project ideas on to this least well known of Hardy's possible loves. (It is even tempting to point out the half resonance between "Cassie" and Tess.)

There is a great conundrum in Hardy's personal life before he met Emma. It appears in the intensity of poems which suggest a love triangle gone wrong, in the ambivalence of Hardy's relationship with Moule, in the themes which recur in his novels. Perhaps it is wrong to link together all these elements. It may be simply that the triangle was among Hardy, Jane Nicholls, and her husband to be; that Moule's supposed son and persistent Dorset rumours that Hardy fathered a "bastard" are unconnected; that Arabella and Father Time have nothing to do with Hardy's life... But many other known events from Hardy's life do emerge in poems and novels. For example, *The Well-Beloved*, in which the Hardy self-caricature Pierston falls in love with three generations of women, *Tess of the Durbervilles* in which Angel ends up with Tess's sister Mary Lou, and *The Hand of Ethelberta* in which Julian ends up marrying his beloved Ethelberta's sister Picotee all suggest something of Hardy's experiences with the Sparks and Nicholls sisters. If there was a triangle among Hardy, Moule, and the woman whose son was hanged in Australia, it may explain much – not least why the details of its history have been so thoroughly suppressed.

A final clue to the conundrum may be found in a poem, "The Place on the Map", which was published in a periodical in 1913 with the subtitle, "A Poor Schoolmaster's Story".

I

I look upon the map that hangs by me –
Its shires and towns and rivers lined in varnished artistry –
And I mark a jutting height
Coloured purple, with a margin of blue sea.

II

– 'Twas a day of latter summer, hot and dry ;
Ay, even the waves seemed drying as we walked on, she and I
By this spot where, calmly quite,
She unfolded what would happen by and by.

III

This hanging map depicts the coast and place,
And re-creates therewith our unforeboded troublous case
All distinctly to my sight,
And her tension, and the aspect of her face.

IV

Weeks and weeks we had loved beneath that blazing blue,
Which had lost the art of raining, as her eyes to-day had too,
While she told what, as by sleight,
Shot our firmament with rays of ruddy hue.

V

For the wonder and the wormwood of the whole
Was that what in realms of reason would have joyed our double soul
Wore a torrid, tragic light
Under order-keeping's rigorous control.

VI

So, the map revives her words, the spot, the time,
And the thing we found we had to face before the next year's prime;
The charted coast stares bright,
And its episode comes back in pantomime.

Lois Deacon supposes the "jutting height" to be Portland Bill, near Weymouth, and that this poem refers to Hardy getting Tryphena pregnant at Weymouth in the summer of 1867. Portland is whitish-grey from its quarries, and it points Southward. Gittings, however, scuppered this argument by proving that in 1867 at Weymouth there were only three clear days in August in one of the wettest and greyest summers on record.

On the other hand, Hardy spent August 1870, in one of the dryest summers of the period, idyllically with Emma Gifford, who was to become his wife, at St Juliot, in Cornwall, where he had met her earlier that year, in February when he came to make drawings for the restoration of the church of which her brother-in-law was vicar. Beeny cliff, near St Juliot, is backed by slopes purple with heather and juts out like a huge black horn into the Atlantic, facing Westward.

Yet there is a chronological snag: Hardy was absent from St Juliot between 11 March and 8 August, so could not have impregnated (or thought he did) Emma in June. Furthermore, he left before the end of August, which leaves only three weeks for impregnation and a pregnancy scare whereas "weeks and weeks" by definition means at least four weeks. Weymouth and an earlier year may win through: the summer of 1869 was notable for its sunniness. In this case, the jutting height is after all Portland Bill, and the couple not Hardy and Emma.

There is surely significance in the subtitle, which has led some critics to suppose that the poem is not about Hardy at all, but about Moule who had been a schoolmaster at Marlborough until leaving abruptly in 1868. In the light of Hardy's other Weymouth poems which clearly tell other parts of the same story, this is certainly Hardy's own story to some extent. If Hardy and Moule are both lovers of the same woman, however, then the subtitle acknowledges that it is also Moule's story. The woman's revelation, perhaps to each separately, would indeed have affected another "double soul" that of Hardy and his friend.

Moule was, however, never "poor" as Hardy himself indisputably was, as a young architect. There is some suggestion in the Weymouth poems that he could not marry his woman because of this or because she saw him as a prospectively poor poet. His very first novel, *The Poor Man and the Lady*, was rejected by a publisher and destroyed. But the poem of the same title which purports to summarise it states the theme clearly: poor man is rejected by society lady with whom he has had an affair but who then marries a more suitable man. Furthermore there are echoes of this in Hardy's first published novel, *Desperate Remedies,* in which an ineligible poor architect hero first kisses the young heroine, Cytherea, in a boat in the waters off Weymouth, and which Hardy began writing that summer.

Moule at one point was trying to help Hardy get a place reading for the Anglican ministry at Cambridge, as Barnes had done. The idea of the free-thinking Hardy (not exactly an atheist, but a sort of gnostic agnostic), who as an old man regaled the young Robert Graves with imitations of bishops taking their tea, becoming a parson seems grotesque, if not hypocritical. But Hardy believed in the necessity of religion (of some sort), and even as an old man would go to church and read the lesson. He may, as often, have justified himself by thinking of Shelley, who said to Peacock (who recorded this in a biography that Hardy knew) that he sometimes thought of entering the church.

> "What", I said, "to become a clergyman with your ideas of the faith?" "Assent to the supernatural part of it", he said, "is merely technical. Of the moral doctrines of Christianity I am a more decided disciple than many of its more ostentatious professors. And consider for a moment how much good a clergyman may do..."

This represents Hardy's thinking exactly. But, like Shelley, he was not actually capable of entering the church. He stayed with architecture, with the main commission of restoring dilapidated churches in that Victorian neo-Gothic style which is now seen as over-restored: in later life Hardy regretted having desecrated churches in this way, though in fact his restoration of St Juliot is lovely. But he knew that to earn a living in society, one must contract with society to do something useful which is not poetry. Eventually, with the strong support of Emma, he was able to cut loose from architecture and contract to do the more creative but also more painful pursuit of writing novels for the public he knew would not read his poetry.

## Emma

The story of Hardy's arrival at St Juliot in Cornwall as a young architect, to do drawings of a decaying church, and his falling in love with the sister-in-law of the parson, is told directly but fragmentally in Hardy's poems after Emma's death, indirectly in *A Girl with Blue Eyes*, and in biographies, where Seymour-Smith's account is the most sympathetic in emphasising that for all her later eccentricities (dogmatic Anglicanism, running Hardy down in public, insisting that planks be put for the cats to walk between chairs), in large part due to their private tragedy of not having children as they had wanted, she was a powerful support to Hardy. She urged him to take the risk of giving up architecture for novel-writing, she copied out his early manuscripts which were discussed at every stage with her, and she eventually consented to his plan of returning to Dorchester to build a house there. (Although, characteristically, he continued to lead a double life between London for the social season, and Dorset where he avoided "county" society in favour of his family of origin and a few country friends, like Hermann Lea). That eventually he alienated her by writing novels she could not approve of, by falling in love with or becoming infatuated with at least three other women (Florence Henniker, Agnes Grove, Florence Dugdale) is neither her fault nor his. Academic biographers, such as Millgate, whose urge is to prove superiority to their subject, may permit themselves to sit in judgement over Hardy and Emma, but why should the rest of us?

There is, however, a knot somewhere in the relationship which proves difficult to identify, let alone untangle. One string in this knot is that Hardy contracted a bladder infection during his honeymoon with Emma (supposedly from swimming in the sea in France, but more likely from what is known as "honeymoonitis") which recurred over the years and once nearly killed him (see the poem "A Wasted Illness"). It is sometimes supposed that this made him sterile, or as country language would have it "impotent", which the academically potent Millgate seizes on as evidence of actual impotence – a bizarre theory given Hardy's poems and novels, the rumours of an illegitimate son, the fact that a physical affair with Florence Dugdale before their marriage is amply documented (not least by his housemaids who, in a position to know, reported that they were sharing a bed in his house within a few months of Emma's death – and he had previously set her up as in effect his kept mistress in a flat in Baker Street in London), the fact that she fretted as late as 1918 (to Siegfried Sassoon) about the possibility of having a child by Hardy when he was too ancient to act as a proper father, and his remark to Edmund Blunden about being sexually capable until the age of 84.

There is no space here to discuss Hardy's frustrated attempt to seduce a society lady with literary aspirations (which he encouraged, against his better judgment), Florence Henniker. One of his known infatuations was with Agnes Grove, with whom he danced an evening away under the trees in 1895 (see the poem "Concerning Agnes"). A recent book of diaries (*The Grove Diaries,* 1995) from the family she married into reveals her as a socialite but a determinedly independent suffragette who nevertheless was always surrounded by adoring young men. At the time, Emma wrote to an acquaintance that aging husbands develop "Eastern ideas of matrimony." Hardy's final infatuation (or love) for the young Dorset actress Gertrude Bugler, when he was aged over 80 and she in her twenties, worried Florence Hardy enough to cause her to ruin Gertrude's acting career through intrigue so that she would be safely tied up in domesticity and not be a temptation for Hardy to run away with her…

After Emma's death in 1912, Hardy, to Florence's chagrin, made several pilgrimages to St Juliot in Cornwall, where he had fallen in love with her in 1870. He had a plaque erected in her honour on the wall of the church he had restored, in the light of their love, between 1870 and 1872. As he approached the church door, on his left he would have seen a newly erected gravestone (he always read the inscriptions) to an "Elizabeth Nicholls", who had died in 1909. Not the same one, of course. But, as he would have put it, one of "life's little ironies."

St Juliot church survives, in the pastoral Valency valley behind Boscastle and not far from the black horn of Beeny cliff plunging into the Atlantic, as the one complete example of Hardy's skill as an architect. It was his first complete restoration, and his last. In spite of a few disasters (the local carpenter proudly destroyed the rood screen Hardy had instructed him to preserve and replaced it with a "better" ersatz one) and his own later regret at having participated in such restorations, Hardy must surely have felt proud of this church. It is on the one hand refreshingly light and (still) new, with immaculate timber roofing, white-washed walls, and a sense of space. And on the other hand, it contains medieval windows whose variations on the Gothic have been sensitively transferred to the new windows which bring in the light, and wood carvings which pick up the motifs of more ancient carvings. The tower he built (on the top of which Elfride from *A Girl with Blue Eyes*, and Emma herself, can be imagined walking dangerously) is in good proportion unlike the similarly restored tower in the neighbouring parish of Lesnewth, which dwarfs its church. The reader who visits Bockhampton and Stinsford may be touched by a sense of Hardy's life and death. But a visit to St Juliot provides more of a sense of his work. The church recalls his novels: due proportion, clarity of line, modernity along with respect for the old, sensitivity to the pre-existing. It is a monument to order. But its position in the peaceful Valency valley is only a mile from the outer world of disorder and terror where Beeny plunges its black horn into the Atlantic.

# 2 Early Poems (1865-1872)

We stood by a pond that winter day,
And the sun was white, as though chidden of God,
And a few leaves lay on the starving sod;
 – They had fallen from an ash, and were gray.

Your eyes on me were as eyes that rove
Over tedious riddles of years ago;
And some words played between us to and fro
 On which lost the more by our love.

The smile on your mouth was the deadest thing
Alive enough to have strength to die;
And a grin of bitterness swept thereby
 Like an ominous bird a-wing…

Since then, keen lessons that love deceives,
And wrings with wrong, have shaped to me
Your face, and the God-curst sun, and a tree,
 And a pond edged with grayish leaves.

"Neutral Tones" was written in 1867, when Hardy was aged 27 and studying architecture in London. Its conciseness, its uncompromising gloom, and the resonance between emotion and landscape are typical of his most personal poems throughout his life, and though there are a few signs of clumsiness ("wrings with wrong") and archaism ("swept thereby") these can be found here and there in his poems almost 60 years later: when he had said what he wanted to say, he never paid much heed to fashion or current taste. It is one of what he later described as "a much larger number which perished", of poems written in London between 1865 and 1867. The surviving others included an exercise in Greek Sapphic metre which seems to describe his friendship with Moule, an art ballad ("Amabel") which seems to describe his disillusioned reunion with Augusta Martin in London, a few short lyrics, and 15 sonnets (including 6 spoken, as it were, as "She to Him") which have sometimes been described for want of a better word as "Shakespearean". One of these is "Her Confession":

As some blind soul, to whom a debtor says
"I'll now repay the amount I owe to you,"
In inward gladness feigns forgetfulness
That such a payment ever was his due
(His long thought notwithstanding), so did I
At our last meeting waive your proffered kiss
With quick divergent talk of scenery nigh,
By such suspension to enhance my bliss.

And as his looks in consternation fall
When, gathering that the debt is lightly deemed,
The debtor makes as not to pay at all,
So faltered I, when your intention seemed

Converted by my false uneagerness
To putting off for ever the caress.

The meticulously developed simile of the debtor repaying the debt is indeed reminiscent of Shakespeare's Sonnets, and Hardy's follows the Shakespearean rhyme scheme (abab cdcd efef gg), but the carry over of the phrasing into the (separated out) final couplet is original, as is the brilliant, and touching, image the couplet states. The sonnet is also psychologically penetrating and sophisticated: not for nothing had Hardy, at the age of 23, filled notebook pages with diagrams, derived from the French socialist thinker François Fourier, of "Human Passion, Mind and Character." This and the other sonnets, with the lyrical poems, such as "Neutral Tones", which seem to be about the same doomed relationship, may be influenced by Hardy's reading of George Meredith's *Modern Life* sequence as well as Shakespeare, but are more original than, at the distance of over 140 years, is immediately obvious.

For comparison, all that is necessary is a trawl through the mid 19th century poems in Quiller-Couch's definitive *Oxford Book of English Verse* (1924). Take a stanza from Tennyson's "Mariana":

Her tears fell with the dews at even;
    Her tears fell ere the dews were dried;
She could not look on the sweet heaven,
    Either at morn or eventide.
After the flitting of the bats,
    When thickest dark did trance the sky,
    She drew her casement-curtain by,

And glanced athwart the glooming flats.
    She only said, 'The night is dreary,
    He cometh not', she said;
She said, 'I am aweary, aweary,
I would that I were dead!'

And this was one of Tennyson's best loved poems! A fatuous musicality, a phoney Gothic setting, a hopelessly artsy diction ("glanced athwart the glooming flats"), a filling in of metrical regularity by redundant syllables ("did trance" instead of tranced or entranced: the use of "did" in this way was one of Shelley's self indulgent habits that was adopted in a whole succeeding century of gush), a total lack of authenticity of feeling: the reader knows very well that Tennyson is not feeling, but playing at it. The verses induce the same queasy sensation in most modern readers as the pseudo-Gothic architecture of Queen Victoria's additions to Windsor Castle, or a painting by Burne Jones – the sensation described by a nuts-and-bolts Australian philosopher, David Stove, as "Horror Victorianorum": Horror of the Victorians.

Or take Browning's

Thus the Mayne glideth
Where my Love abideth;
Sleep's no softer: it proceeds
On through lawns, on through meads,
On and on, whate'er befall,
Meandering and musical,
Though the niggard pasturage
Bears not on its shaven ledge
Aught but weeds and waving grasses. . .

The same utter emptiness and phoniness. And Tennyson and Browning were the big guns! As Hardy wrote in later life (1922):

The bower we shrined to Tennyson,
    Gentlemen,
Is roof-wrecked; damps there drip upon
Sagged seats, the creeper nails are rust,
    The spider is sole denizen...

But to Quiller-Couch, as late as 1924, Tennyson's bower was far from wrecked. Victorian horrors were present around Hardy for all of his long life. They even infected him at times. But it is remarkable how only a few of his very earliest poems (and none after the early 1870s) contain "thees" and "thous" – that revolting 19th century diction which, it must be admitted, had its origin in the high-flown romanticism of Coleridge and Shelley, and which survived long enough to incapacitate the poems even of the talented American poet, Trumbull Stickney (1874-1904), though Stickney's contemporary Robert Frost, who read Hardy avidly, and only began publishing late, was able to leave them behind.

Hardy's use of language was original from the start for its mixture of archaisms, modernisms, and coinages. Or perhaps it is incorrect to write of a poet's use of language: rather, language uses him or her. As Pasternak realised excitedly in his youth, the poet is not the author of his poem, he is its subject and the poem's title is its surname! And "I didn't care at all what name was given to the force which produced the book, since that force was immeasurably greater than I and the notions of poetry around me." At any rate, it is worth noting that what may irritate in Hardy's language – such archaisms as "blooth" for blossom, or the outrageous "greenth" for green – is a sign of his openness to inspiration. As Pasternak (more willing to discuss the processes of poetry than Hardy) put it, "I wrote down only what by the character of the language or by the turn of phrase seemed to escape me entirely of its own accord." A more watchful, guarded poet would never have admitted such terms as Hardy did to consciousness. But nor would he have admitted such oddities as "chidden of God." Which means, in standard English, "chided by God." But apart from the ugly assonance that would occur between "chided" and "by", "chidden" is perfect in its hints at similar words, closer to the Anglo-Saxon than the standardised "chided", such as "hidden" and "ridden" which somehow suggest use, and waste.

It must be emphasised that Hardy, as a poet rather than a novelist, was taken seriously by no one until the First World War poets Blunden, Sassoon and Graves beat a path to his door after 1918. (A few poems he sent to periodicals about the Boer War and the First World War did receive attention, but these are exceptions which prove the rule). He sent various poems out in the 1860s from Westbourne Park Villas to London periodicals, but not a single one was accepted – understandably, since what passed for poetry, as quoted above, had no resemblance either to Hardy's poems or to any other "real" poems then being written – the conspicuous example being Gerald Manley Hopkins who also wrote for his desk drawer, and whose poems were not published until 1918, long after his death, when the Victorian horrors had been blasted away by the new horrors of the First World War. Hardy put his early poems aside (though he transformed a few to prose passages in early novels), and they only appeared in *Wessex Poems*, in 1898. Though he had by then published all his novels, and was a Great Writer, this first book of poems, illustrated with 31 of his own drawings, was nastily reviewed and sold only a few hundred copies. His next book *Poems of the Past and Present* (1902) sold somewhat better but still the critical consensus was that Hardy should have stuck to novels.

The bibliography of Hardy's early poems (which are defined here as those written before the publication of his first novel in 1871) is therefore complicated. They appeared in collections in 1898, 1902, 1909, 1916, 1917, 1922, 1925, and posthumously in 1928. A particular collection usually contains a mixture of new poems and of old poems from pre-1898 which are sometimes given a date and a place, sometimes a date or a place only, but sometimes no indication that they are not new – and they may have been revised or rewritten. The dating of Hardy's early poems is thus often from internal evidence, or a combination of this and such external evidence as he chooses to give.

A further complicating factor is that those early poems which Hardy does choose to date are from the 1860s and 70s, but almost never from the 1880s and 90s when, although in the throes of novel writing, he did write at least some poems. He seems to have preferred to keep the dates secret, given that he was married to Emma but some of the poems are about other women.

Most of the poems written at Westbourne Park Villas are dated by Hardy, and form two identifiable clusters, the first in *Wessex Poems* (1898), the second in the section More Love Lyrics in *Time's Laughingstocks* (1909). There is one other conspicuously identifiable cluster of early poems, set in Weymouth between 1869 and 1871 (some dated and placed, some belonging with them by inference) mostly also included in the remarkable 25 poems of More Love Lyrics. With the 9 London sonnets from Wessex Poems, and "Neutral Tones" this amounts to 34 poems (there is an intruder in the form of a poem to Emma Hardy – see below) which are clearly intertwined in tone and theme, and are either to two separate women – one of them possibly an actress in London, and one of them a young woman in Weymouth with whom Hardy has clearly had a love affair (one poem even describes him waking up next to her) but who has been pressured by her father into marrying another, more suitable man – or to the same woman who was both an actress in London and from Weymouth. This may seem a far fetched combination, but there was (and still is) a theatre in Weymouth to which London actresses came, and in Hardy's novel *The Trumpet Major*, the anti-heroine Matilda is just such an actress (as well as a semi-prostitute) who moves between Weymouth and London.

Or perhaps these are poems about Hardy's chagrin at being supplanted in a genuine love affair with Jane Nicholls, by her respectable husband to be, the aptly named (given the context) Mr Beach. Or perhaps they are about Cassie Pole (see Chapter 1), about whom we know next to nothing.

That there was something Hardy wished to hide about this relationship is evident from his dispersal of its poems here and there in his works, his only sporadic provision of dates and places, and his cunning placement of a poem obviously to his wife Emma, "The Division", with the date 1893 provided, among More Love Poems, as a kind of decoy: it even addresses her as "Dear", as some of the Weymouth poems address their recipient.

One poem which perhaps sums up the Weymouth relationship is "Four Footprints:

Here are the tracks upon the sand
Where stood last evening she and I –
Pressed heart to heart, and hand to hand;
The morning sun has baked them dry.

I kissed her wet face – wet with rain,
For arid grief had burnt up tears,
While reached us as in sleeping pain
The distant gurgling of the weirs.

"I have married him – yes; feel that ring;
'Tis a week ago that he put it on...
A dutiful daughter does this thing,
And resignation succeeds anon!

"But that I body and soul was yours
Ere he'd possession, he'll never know.
He's a confident man. 'The husband scores,'
He says, 'in the long run' ...Now, Dear, go!"

I went. And to-day I pass the spot;
It is only a smart the more to endure;
And she whom I held is as though she were not,
For they have resumed their honeymoon tour.

This is undated, but comes just after the poem dated Weymouth 1869 in which he describes waking next to his beloved and in "an insight that would not die" (Hardy had many of these), seeing her as "but one / of the common crowd." It may of course have been worked on, but its origin in the Weymouth cluster is indisputable. This is a poem probably written when Hardy was aged 29, and it is too naive to count among the best of the poems written across more than five decades, but it shares their characteristics: a narrative told with simple clarity, a scene which evokes and echoes a couple's feelings, a dialogue of painful realism, some touches of clumsiness which somehow fall into place as part of the human condition, an unabashed use of old-fashioned words (eg "anon") but only when no current word with the same meaning exists, and a poignant, elegiac sense of loss. (But then, as a modern American poet and critic Rosanna Warren has pointed out in a study of elegy, all lyrical poems of feeling are elegiac). We take the technical side of these characteristics (the mixing of narrative and dialogue, the down to earth clarity) for granted now: in lesser hands than Hardy's they are the commonplace mannerisms of the 20th century poetry in English which he played a key but usually unacknowledged role in setting up.

One vein which can be found in even the earliest of Hardy's poems, and is unfairly overshadowed for some readers by the intensity of the vein of gloom, is humour. Examples are "The Ruined Maid" and "Reminiscences of a Dancing Man" with its descriptions of dance-halls, Almack's, Willis's, Cremorne, which were in effect brothels, which begins mock heroically:

Who now remembers Almack's balls –
        Willis's sometime named –
In those two smooth-floored upper halls
        For faded ones so famed?
Where as we trod to trilling sound
The fancied phantoms stood around...

The very early long poem, "The Bride-Night Fire", 1866, is remarkable not only for its humour but its being written in Dorset dialect. Hardy already knew William Barnes (they spoke in dialect together), and the poem is an exploration of a language he might have wanted to, but decided not to, pursue farther. He has to annotate "The Bride-Night Fire" to make it comprehensible, but it is worth reading, for the light touch of its humorous descriptions (some of which he felt he had to bowdlerize for publication), such as when Tim Tankens rescues his beloved Barbree from the fire of the house she has gone to for her wedding night with the prosperous husband (a tranter, or carter) she loathes, "Her cwold little buzzums half-naked he views / Played about by the frolicsome breeze, / Her light tripping totties, her ten little tooes…" and for moments which succeed in being both farcical and moving (a combination rarely found except in Shakespeare comedy, and here and there in Hardy's novels), as when the villagers search the ruined house for its owner:

> "Where's the tranter? " said men and boys ; "where can he be?"
> "Where's the tranter?" said Barbree alone.
> "Where on e'th is the tranter?" said everybod-y:
> They sifted the dust of his perished roof tree,
> And all they could find was a bone.

These early poems repay study: they already contain the true Hardy. How he managed to live with this in himself in the nauseating Victorian cultural world he inhabited is a clue to how he managed his life and his novels by basing them in that other world, partly of his own, partly of his neighbours, and now partly of all his readers, which he called Wessex.

# 3 Novels of Ingenuity

## *Desperate Remedies* (1871), *The Hand of Ethelberta* (1875), *A Laodicean* (1881)

In his General Preface to the Wessex Edition of his complete novels, in 1912, Hardy set out a classification in which he included all of them as "Wessex Novels", but sorted them into three groups: Novels of Character and Environment, which "approach most nearly to uninfluenced works" (ie he considered them the most original), Romances and Fantasies, and Novels of Ingenuity, which "show a not infrequent disregard of the probable in the chain of events, and depend for their interest mainly on the incidents themselves." There is some disingenuousness in the remark on "the probable", which is in fact neglected in all Hardy's novels. But the Novels of Ingenuity, which he also described as "Experiments", are consciously in the "sensation novel" tradition of the mid nineteenth century, most successfully exemplified in the novels of Wilkie Collins (*The Moonstone, The Lady in White,* etc.) in which fiendishly intricate plots are more important than delineation of character (although Collins at his best was no slouch at this either) or than the natural development of a story. (A plot is more calculated and artificial than a story, even a made-up story.) These novels were also written relatively early in Hardy's career.

But Hardy's development as a novelist was not linear. Even the three Novels of Ingenuity are interspaced with early examples of the other kinds, and even at the very end of his novelistic career, after a series of Novels of Character and Circumstance (those we know best) he finished up with the outrageously unrealistic *The Well-Beloved,* which belongs among Romances and Fantasies.

### *Desperate Remedies*

*Desperate Remedies* was Hardy's first novel, published at his own expense (as was common). The first edition of 500 copies was soon remaindered, and he recouped only £59 of his £75 costs. It was snuffed out, as Hardy saw it, by one brutal review in *The Spectator,* and was not saved by a favourable review elsewhere from his friend Moule. It only began to do relatively well when republished 17 years later, when he was famous. However, almost all critics now agree that it contains powerful passages and images, and its sensationalism is less jarring as time passes: it was in fact a daring first novel. (Though its unpublished and now lost predecessor *The Poor Man and the Lady*, an avowedly socialistic attack on the upper classes, may have been more daring.)

It is also clearly a novel by a poet. This is at once apparent in Hardy's use of names, which bears close examination in all his novels. Admittedly, most Victorian novels followed the picaresque and theatre (see Ben Jonson, above all) tradition of naming characters in amusing or relevant ways. (The practice was not like that of the 20th century Simenon, who began all his novels by collecting names for characters at random from a telephone directory.) Dickens's schoolmaster Mr Thwackum, the sycophantic Uriah Heep, the decent boy Steerforth, the sadistic Mr Murdstone (Murd = Fr. "merde") and others continue the line of the 18th century novelist Fielding's innocent Parson Adams and the wicked Lord Fellamar (suggestions of fellatio, of "fell" meaning evil, and falling and marring of – and of "love skin" as an old word for skin, plus Latin "amare"). But although Hardy sometimes used picaresque names (eg Lovejoy) or stock rustic names (Poorgrass) or noble names (Lord Luxellian), his names often suggest allusions which help explain characteristics or themes not overtly mentioned in the novel – part of its subtext, as it were.

The title of *Desperate Remedies* is itself an allusion to Hardy's need to enter the literary marketplace where *The Poor Man and the Lady* had failed, by writing a "sensation novel". Its heroine and its anti-heroine, who turns out to have had an affair with the heroine's father are both called Cytherea, the name for Aphrodite (Venus) as she emerges from the foam in rebirth, and in Cytherea the younger Cytherea the elder (who dies at the end of the novel) is in a sense reborn. The villain, the elder Cytherea's bastard son, is called Aeneas Manston: he sees himself as a kind of conquering hero, an Aeneas (son of Venus Cytherea) but all he conquers is people, through seduction and manipulation. He is a failure. The name emphasises his upside down nature, and also a hint of foreignness (he is dark and Mediterranean-looking). He is also a "man stone", ie a tombstone. By contrast, the fair-haired young hero is Edward Springrove, his names typical of the Anglo-Saxon farming stock (Hardy was quite self-consciously a "Saxon" from Wessex, after all, "West Saxony"), and suggesting life and Spring – Venus Cytherea's season. Also Spring-rove, with a connotation of a potential sexual adventurer, and a sacred grove, so that he and Cytherea match each other.

The story is indeed set out as a plot, with chapter headings spelled out

("August the Ninth. One to Two o'Clock a.m."). It fulfils its mission as a sensation novel, and the plot will not be given away here: it includes many mistaken identities, and brilliantly described scenes – the Three Tranters Inn that burns down leaving forensic evidence that a guest has been reduced to ashes, an idyllic first kiss in a rowboat on a summer evening, which could come out of one of the Weymouth poems (and no doubt is autobiographical: Cytherea, with whom Eliza Nicholls is said to have identified herself, remarks when Springrove confesses he has written poems, that "the difference between a common man and a recognised poet is, that one has been deluded, and cured of his delusion, and the other continues deluded all his days"), and most extraordinarily a scene in which Miss Aldclyffe (Cytherea the elder) invites Cytherea the younger, whom she has employed as a personal maid, to bed with her, and clasps and kisses her while wheedling confidences out of her. When Cytherea admits she is in love (with Springrove), Miss Aldclyffe

> changed her tone with fitful rapidity. 'Cytherea, try to love me more than you love him – do. I love you more sincerely than any man can. Do, Cythie: don't let any man stand between us. O, I can't bear that!' She clasped Cytherea's neck again.

This is a fully fledged Lesbian scene, as most critics have realised, although some suppose it is unconscious on the part of the naive bumpkin Hardy, or that at best it must have been taken from anecdotes from his Sparks cousins "in service" to tyrannical mistresses. But it is a mistake to assume Hardy was sexually naive, or needed second hand information: a knowledge of sexual realities permeates all his novels, whether stated obliquely but certainly as in *Tess of the Durbervilles*, or frankly joked about through outrageous double-meanings as in *Two on a Tower*. There may, of course, be something of Hardy's own childhood experience with Augusta Martin in this scene. But it stands as a valid description of how two lonely, sexually frustrated (about men) women can first comfort, then excite each other in bed. And the novel eventually adds yet another sensational dimension: this Lesbian encounter is between two women who have loved the same man, one sexually, one as his daughter.

From the beginning the novel is one of poetic images. In the first chapter Cytherea watches helplessly as her father, an architect, plunges to his death in a fall from a church *spire* and it has been made clear that he has been frustrated in his a*spir*ations in life and love: his death fall hints at the orgasm which has created Cytherea and which has not been often repeated. Later, after the cuddle in bed between the two Cythereas, when Cytherea the younger has returned to her bed, she is awakened by a distant rattling sound, then the barking of dogs: the old baronet Aldclyffe has just died, and though the scene like many others in the novel is "Gothic", again hints at orgasm, as the love-death which might have been enjoyed by the two Cythereas or postponed.

The danger for a poet novelist, though, is that the ideas for novels form a series of images which must then be connected by an artificial story line. Hence Hardy's too apparent struggle with his plot. He also adopted what he seems to have thought was the necessary persona of the novelist (he may have cribbed this from George Eliot: he was not averse to picking up techniques from successful practitioners of the craft in which he intended to make a living) in making frequent generalisations about the rules of life – extrapolating, not always without interest, but always inappropriately, from that minute particular which is the stuff of poetry and also, as he eventually had the confidence to realise, of realistic novels. At best these *sententiae* are insightful as, "Perhaps, indeed, the only bliss in the course of love which can truly be called Eden-like is that which prevails immediately after doubt has ended and before reflection has set in at the dawn of the emotion, when it is not recognised by name..." At worst they are bad and pompous psychology as, "Pity for one's self for being wasted is mostly present in these moods of abnegation."

The minute particular is, however, often powerfully present: "the melancholy red leaves, lying thickly in the channels by the roadside, ever and anon loudly tapped on by heavy drops of water, which the boughs above had collected from the foggy air."

*Desperate Remedies* contains in pristine form much of Hardy's thinking. Some of this is unoriginal for his time: for instance, he believes without question in heredity, so that Manston inevitably shares the weaknesses of his mother. But of course now, at the start of the 21st century we have come full circle: after a century of horrors in believing fascistically that we can change ourselves, at will, and others, we have come back to our limitations. Some of Hardy's thought is overtly radical. How many people in the nineteenth century would be capable of thinking, let alone writing, that "the fact remains that, after all, women are Mankind, and that in many of the sentiments of life the difference of sex is but a difference of degree"? Hardy, who had already resolved, in his London days, to live life "as an emotion, rather than… as a science of climbing", emphasises in *Desperate Remedies* that women and men, in spite of their differences, can share identical ideas and emotions, which at any rate he sees as identical: "the ideas, or rather emotions."

It also contains much of the animism so typical of Hardy. His counterpart to Pasternak's cabbages blue with cold is the "rank broad leaves – the sensuous natures of the vegetable world." Along with animism comes a faith in coincidence. As Hardy puts it rather coyly in one of his *sententiae*, "To see persons looking with children's eyes at any ordinary scenery is a proof that they possess the charming facility of drawing new sensations from an old experience." But once a person is sensitive in this way, connections are made between experiences. And emotions actually create experience. In *Desperate Remedies,* Hardy is always rational about coincidence: it is either overtly explained as illusion, or it springs from the emotions which make people act: Manston, for example, creates a series of mistakes and coincidences from a misreading of his Bradshaw (the Victorian railway timetable), but this misreading is due to his emotional predisposition. For Hardy, thoughts are things: they can produce material events as surely as can physical actions. For example, Farmer Springrove (Edward's father) is about to bolt the Inn door on what turns out to be the night of the fire, "when the idea struck him that there was just a possibility of his son's return by the latest train… The old man thereupon left the door unfastened" – a crucial event in the story.

There is as much of Hardy in Manston as, more obviously, in Springrove. Manston sees Cytherea (born in foam, after all) as "a lovely Nothing" a thought worthy of one of Hardy's poems. And the final paragraph of Manston's last letter states a theme Hardy often came back to in poems (eg "Dead Man Walking"): "I am now about to enter on my normal condition. For people are almost always in their graves. When we survey the long race of men, it's strange and still more strange to find that they are mainly dead men, who have scarcely ever been otherwise."

Critics who emphasise the unoriginality of Hardy's stage-villains – Manston, Damon Wildeve, Alec Durberville, all described in stock terms, dark and sensual lipped, Don Juanesque – seem to miss the point that these are in part necessary vehicles for Hardy's own dark side. Overtly, Springrove, Clym Yeobright, and Angel Clare, the naive of this earth, tending to blondness (Hardy was fair) and idealism, express many of Hardy's hopes. But covertly, his villains express his fears, his cynicism, his ruthlessness. (As Seymour-Smith has remarked, Hardy seems to have been "an accomplished seducer.") The contrast is best worked through in *The Woodlanders*, his own favourite novel, between Fitzpiers, a very subtle kind of villain complete with many virtues, and Winterbourne, an equally subtle kind of hero with many faults. But it is already potent in *Desperate Remedies.*

Finally, Cytherea, although the tyranny of the "ingenious" plot causes her practically to disappear from the action for much of the second half of the novel, as Hardy's first novel heroine sets the pattern for those who follow. She is, like the others, more engaging than any of the male characters who either prey on her or cherish her – who, in either case, want to possess her. Hardy does not appropriate his heroines. Close as Hardy comes to Cytherea, or Bathsheba, or Grace, or Tess, and much as he enters into their thoughts, he always seems to be perceiving them from outside which, as a man, he most naturally does. But he does dwell on them, wanting to possess them lingeringly: he is nothing less than in love with them.

## *The Hand of Ethelberta*

*The Hand of Ethelberta* may be the least loved of Hardy's novels, in part because the reader's impulse to romance, which has been cynically tickled throughout with the hope that the somewhat insipid composer of music Christopher Julian will finally succeed in capturing the independent-minded Ethelberta, is frustrated at the end: Ethelberta makes a realistic marriage to a nobleman who gives her his title then dies, on which she takes up a career as a reader of her own stories, and Christopher is fobbed off with her sweet little sister Picotee. This is one denouement it is not necessary to keep from the prospective reader: the ending of this novel has no rewards except material ones, for Ethelberta. Here too Hardy is being radical: as good as stating that an independent career for a woman, or failing that a successfully manipulated alliance with a rich sucker, is preferable to romance, any day. The problem is, he is also being as cold as Ethelberta herself. Millgate claims that she is in some sense a surrogate for Hardy himself, and he may be right but it is difficult to care. Unlike all Hardy's other novels, *The Hand of Ethelberta* is strangely monotone and linear. The characters manipulate each other, while Hardy manipulates them. The only one who comes alive is the sad little Picotee, whom Hardy neglects as much as his characters do. The novel contains no surprises, and is like one of those think-pieces which so disappoint when encountered among Hardy's poems.

It is the least poetic of the novels. And perhaps for this reason, it was necessary for Hardy to write. (But for a valiant attempt to pull the best out of this novel, see the poet Seymour-Smith's discussion in his biography of Hardy.) Even his wife seems not to have opened her inscribed copy: the pages were uncut at her death.

The names, as usual, provide some clues to Hardy's intentions. Christopher Julian with its Christian-Roman connotations suggests a certain po-faced rectitude, and Ethelberta (in Anglo-Saxon, "the noble bright") is appropriately sterling stuff. The name Picotee (presumably based on the stream of that name in Dorset) is as delightful, yet light-weight, as its character. The most outrageous name is that of Alfred Neigh – a fashionably neighing and naying pseudo gentleman whose riches stem from his father's business as a knacker (a slaughterer of horses).

Hardy's contempt for the pseudo upper classes in this novel is total: Ethelberta and her butler father (shades possibly of Cassie Pole and her father) run rings around them. In life he always showed some tolerance for the real upper classes (he liked the fact that Lord Portsmouth spoke with a broad West country accent) but he seems to have loathed parvenus more than any other social species, and rejected trying to become one himself. He kept his Dorset accent and what was described as a "rough" appearance all through his novel writing career, and only became relatively genteel after his late 50s when he shaved off his beard and, eventually resembling "an ancient moulting eagle", developed a more refined manner which was in its own way rebellious: when he should have been cultivating smoothness as an up and coming novelist, he made a point of being rough, and when he could have got away with a certain roughness in his Dorchester retreat, he became refined, which the locals found offensive.

At the very least, *The Hand of Ethelberta* is evidence of Hardy's social acuity, and should have laid to rest the country bumpkin image which nevertheless remains dear to his sophisticated critics. The dialogue is highly mannered, almost Sheridanesque. There are few descriptions of "the minute particular." Perhaps it is only possible to appreciate the novel by turning our expectations of Hardy, formed by his other novels, on their heads and accepting that it depicts a completely other world – one of complete Victorian utilitarianism, as if Hardy needed to get John Stuart Mill out of his system, and not, unfortunately, with tongue in cheek either. (He had heard Mill speak at a rally, and claimed to know *On Liberty* by heart). "The ingenious Ethelberta" (we must not forget that this is one of the novels of Ingenuity) models her life on Mill's *Utilitarianism*, which she cites at length to justify her unromantic choices for the sake of her family: "As between his own happiness and that of others, utilitarianism requires him to be as strictly impartial as a disinterested and benevolent spectator ..."

In this novel, Hardy's *sententiae*, which he eventually in later novels abandoned and not too soon for most readers, are actually among the best parts. For example, "that complete divorce between thinking and saying which is the hallmark of high civilisation." This is, above all, a highly intellectual novel. Its feminism (Hardy was always a feminist, though he usually expressed this through his *feeling* for a woman's predicament) even is intellectual. Points are made about the problems of women having to speak "men's" language which are radical even today. As Ethelberta says,

> But don't you go believing in sayings, Picotee: they are all made by men, for their own advantages. Women who use public proverbs as a guide through events are those who have not ingenuity enough to make private ones as each event occurs.

Here, with some sense of irony (but it is difficult to detect what is ironic and what not in this novel) Hardy is warning against his own habit of generalisation... It is as if he is not sure of his stance. He referred to the novel as "somewhat frivolous" and "a comedy", but it is hardly comic. One of the few lingering images from the novel is of the several encounters between the sad Julian and the sad Picotee on a bleak path across the heathland behind Bournemouth: it is the only touch which reminds of Hardy's poetry. It is as if the novel hovers on the edge of being a tragedy, but Hardy is determined that it should not be. He actually excised, in revising the novel for the Wessex edition over 30 years after it was written, a quite remarkable sentence spoken by Ethelberta towards the end: "God has got me in his power at last, and is going to scourge me for my bad doings – that's what it seems like." As Gittings points out, this "looks forward to some aspects of Tess." But Hardy seems to have wished to express in Ethelberta the possibility of a woman realising a ruthless independence. The weakness of the novel is that this is an ideological quest. By the time he wrote *Tess of the Durbervilles* he seems to have realised that it was premature: for the foreseeable future, woman would be a victim of all men, and even (as Hardy could not help seeing in his poems of agonised remorse about Emma) of poets.

### *A Laodicean*

*A Laodicean* was dictated by Hardy to Emma when he was at death's door during an illness, and so can be supposed to contain some themes which touched him, but its Novel of Ingenuity format, and its overt intellectuality have tended to alienate readers conditioned to his later Wessex novels. In keeping with his lack of linear progress, it was written after *Under the Greenwood Tree, Far from the Madding Crowd*, and *The Return of the Native*, and even its first readers (Victorian readers of novels published first in magazine serial then in book form, no less than modern movie-goers, liked the expected) must have asked themselves what he was doing returning to the sensation novel. But he needed to write this extraordinary book: his Novels of Character and Circumstance are usually set in the past, but he made a point of describing *A Laodicean* in its subtitle as "A Story of To-day." Like *The Hand of Ethelberta* it tackles the issues of feminism and "the great modern fluctuation of classes and creeds", but it does so with more warmth, and less aridly.

As always the names give a clue. First, a Laodicean is a person who is lukewarm in his or her approach to life or religion: the term comes from the Book of Revelations, and St Paul's reprimand of the inhabitants of Laodicea, for their lack of commitment and faith. In the first scene of the novel, the heroine, Paula Powers – heiress to the fortune of a railway-building father who has left her a castle he has bought which originally belonged to an old family, the de Stancys – is observed voyeuristically by a young architect, George Somerset, as she refuses baptism by immersion in a non-conformist church, and is indirectly rebuked from the pulpit in a sermon about the Laodiceans. (But the paradox is that in her refusal of this baptism, she is anything but a Laodicean.) In the last scene, Paula – married to George after undergoing the tribulations of a plot including mistaken identities, faked photographs, an unscrupulous pursuit by a decadent scion of the de Stancys, and the suicide of a baby-face villain called Dare (an illegitimate de Stancy) – uses the term "Laodicean" one last time to tease him. (But here the paradox is, as Seymour-Smith points out, that she is acknowledging their sexual hotness for each other). In fact, with somewhat clumsy irony (which is nevertheless often missed: as in the other novels of Ingenuity, this is partly Hardy's fault for inconsistency in tone), everyone in the novel is a Laodicean except the protagonists, Paula, George and Dare.

Paula, of course, invokes St Paul: the implication is, surely, that she is *not* a Laodicean, although she seems so by her reluctance to marry Somerset while she plays a game of power politics with the de Stancys. In fact her conflict is precisely St Paul's: whether to marry or burn. But she knows what she wants. She is also Paula *Powers,* and although there is an illusion here to her family's command of money and industrial energy, she is very much concerned with not losing her powers as a woman. That these are real is demonstrated in the novel's denouement where she actively pursues George, who has abandoned hope of her, eventually nabbing him on the top of a church tower in Normandy. It is probably not insignificant that the names Paula and Powers are both of Norman origin in England: Paula is deliberately a modern figure, as opposed to the Saxon George (St George etc.) Somerset. Since the castle of the de Stancys (another Norman name) is supposedly near "Toneborough" (Taunton, in Somerset), George represents the true-blue Englishman, a man of primal decency. One of his problems, even, is that he takes Paula's temporizing no for an answer and will not indulge in the devious intrigue of the Stancys: he will not manipulate events in order to have her, and so almost loses her.

The name Dare may have a connotation further than its obvious one. Shelley once had a pot-shot taken at him by a would-be assassin in North Wales, while living in a house rented from a man called Dare. Perhaps Hardy had heard of this... The character Dare carries a revolver...

Dare is a deliberate manipulator of Chance – a main theme in the novel, and an obsession of Hardy's all the way through to *Tess of the Durbervilles* and *Jude the Obscure*. He is mentioned to be studying a book, Moivré's *Doctrine of Chances*, in order to succeed in gambling. But he does not succeed and this is an important point. Hardy does not, in fact, believe in laws of Chance. He believes that Chance is a result of actions ultimately due to a person's character. Somerset is too decent, when framed (literally) by Dare who doctors a photograph to make Somerset appear dissolute and drunk and conveys this to Paula, to pursue the matter with the police. This decency, a naive lack of suspicion, almost leads him and Paula to disaster. (Similarly, Tess and Jude are naive). Hardy implies that character meets its doom at the hands of Chance, at those moments (determined by the timing of the character's actions) when it loses control of events. This can be positive, as with love, but also negative, as with evil.

Finally, Paula has a strong character, but this is for a while in doubt (is she, after all, a Laodicean?). As Dare remarks, she is reduced to having only "steam powers" – the powers given to her by her inheritance. But

Hardy is interested in her more primitive powers. This is spelled out when the decadent (but ultimately decent: at the limit he is English after all) De Stancy, as he is spying on Paula at her gymnastic exercises (in a pink skin tight suit: this is the second scene of voyeurism in the novel, contrasting with the first, more innocent one, when Somerset spies on her failed baptism) sees her as a "Bona Dea" – an ancient Goddess figure. Her inheritance of "steam powers", and of a castle bought from the rotten aristocracy (whom as usual Hardy despises) is less important in the novel than the question of whether she will use her more primitive powers as a woman, of which everyone from the well-meaning Baptist preacher to the villainous Dare and the decaying de Stancys and even, she fears, Somerset wishes to deprive her. Finally, she does use her powers: she rejects the intrigue around her, successfully pursues Somerset and marries him on her terms – and the castle is burned to the ground by Dare, which does not bother her in the least. She has proved that she can, in fact, take the plunge. She has rejected the baptismal pool which would have swallowed her into Christianity, and which is described as cool and black as *night*, in effect – and the offer of an entry into the aristocracy through marriage to de Stancy, who is a *knight.*

Hardy's social values in *A Laodicean* could not be more clear: he respects solid English country virtues, has no time whatsoever for the "worn out" aristocracy, and although he is aware that the nouveaux riches are simply upstarts, is prepared to give them their due: after all, he was something of a nouveau riche himself.

But his personal values are of more interest. In Paula he is trying to depict a woman of "to-day" who manages to use her powers both ancient and modern, and the implication is that without ancient powers of resolution and desire, modern powers of resources and money do not count for much. Paula is as alive and fascinating as any of Hardy's doomed victim heroines, although she may be less romantic for the fact that she wins through.

All three of Hardy's Novels of Ingenuity are concerned with women who, by their own terms at least, do succeed in getting what they want. Of peculiar interest is the fact that all three novels explore to some extent the way in which women of drive and passion lack a language to enable them to reach their goals. Cytherea is intelligent but mute in expressing her demands. (Like Eliza Nicholls? The "He and She" poems suggest this powerful muteness in "She".) Ethelberta is sharply aware of the lack in a man's world of a language specifically for women. Paula's seeming Laodiceanism (lukewarmness) is her only option in the lack of an acceptable language, for a Victorian young woman, to express what Hardy has made apparent: that far from being lukewarm, she has the hots for Somerset from the moment she sees him, she wants to gobble him up and have him for herself sexually, Bona Dea that she is. But the only languages her environment provides are the Christian one of the well- meaning but out of touch Baptists, the commercial one (adopted greedily by the falling aristocrats the de Stancys) of possible marriage transactions, and the tongue-tied and schoolboyish half-expressions of the architect Somerset. No wonder she takes the only option which preserves her independence: she keeps quiet – as so many of Hardy's heroines ultimately do.

# 4 Romances and Fantasies

***A Pair of Blue Eyes* (1873), *The Trumpet-Major* (1880), *Two on a Tower* (1882), *The Well-beloved* (1897)**

If readers wonder to what extent Hardy wrote ironically, with tongue in cheek (he "means mischief", as one of his first publishers said), his labelling of these four novels as Romances and Fantasies should give a clue: in both *A Pair of Blue Eyes* and *Two on a Tower* a heroine who has been brought as alive as any of Hardy's heroines dies a wretched death, and *The Well-beloved* is a morbid self-dissection. Only *The Trumpet Major* ends "happily" in the marriage of the heroine to one of two brothers – but the other brother, the trumpet major himself, goes off in the last sentence to the Napoleonic wars "to blow his trumpet till silenced for ever upon one of the bloody battle-fields of Spain." Perhaps a rearrangement of the words to "Fantasies of Romance" would be more appropriate: there are romantic, touching, passionate scenes in these novels, but the characters are, as in the title of one of Hardy's volumes of poems, *Time's Laughingstocks*.

## *A Pair of Blue Eyes*

*A Pair of Blue Eyes* is an early novel, Hardy's third, and was well received, but it shows signs of being put together in a hurry. The integration of pure chunks of autobiography (the characters of the young architect Stephen Smith and his upwardly mobile peasant father being based on Hardy and his father, the scene based on St Juliot where he had met Emma, the heroine Elfride in many ways Emma-like, Stephen's rival Henry Knight in many ways Moule-like) with fictional invention is not complete, so that the novel is not so much an objective correlative for Hardy's experience, as a "subjective relative": it does not quite achieve a self-hood of its own. It survives not so much as a whole as through a few intensely realised scenes, such as the famous one where the pompous and emotionally stunted Knight hangs by his fingernails from a cliff face he has slipped over, contemplating a tiny fossil which happens to be in front of his eyes, while the virginal Elfride retreats to strip off her underclothes to tie into a rope to rescue him.

Elfride, as her name suggests, is almost a pre-Raphaelite heroine, elfin, medieval, not robust enough to survive the Victorian world. Knight not only defeats Elfride brutally at chess, he moves like a chess-knight, never directly, always sideways before forward, or vice versa, like a logician. And there is an echo of a description written in later life by Emma – but perhaps the image was current between them much earlier, when she helped him with the manuscript of this novel – of how Hardy's journey to St Juliot for his first visit was in the form of a "knight's move." It is probably too facile to claim that Knight is entirely Moule-like. (Moule reviewed the novel favourably, so presumably did not recognise himself). He is also like a side of Hardy – the intellectual, controlling side, the prose man (faced with the lovely blue-eyed Elfride, Knight states that he prefers hazel eyes!) and rationalist, as opposed to the naive, poetic side represented in the simply named Stephen Smith. Yet again we find two male characters, the light and dark sides of Hardy as it were, having respectively an Anglo-Saxon name (Stephen Smith) and a Norman one (Henry Knight: though "knight" itself is Anglo-Saxon it has a Norman connotation).

Stephen is not ruthless enough to prevail over Elfride's timidity. Knight crushes her intellectually. She is left to be married to Lord Luxellian, and dies at the end, in childbirth, the implication being that perhaps she would have survived childbirth if the father had been Stephen: he is described as fine and senstive, more like her than his rivals. But, grimly, she is defeated by them all: each in his way wants to control her and own her although Hardy is generous enough, and realistic enough about sex (after all, Luxellian is the one who has actually had her in that sense) to allow Smith and Knight to admit forlornly at the end that Luxellian has been "nearer to her than we."

In all Hardy's novels his attitude to the "worn-out" aristocracy and to its sycophantic backers in the Anglican church is nothing less than savage. Parson Swancourt, Elfride's father (perhaps modelled on Emma's beloved uncle who was an Archdeacon as well as on her hypochondriacal brother-in-law the Rector of St Juliot's), is a deceitful, snobbish wastrel who cruises through life in supreme self-satisfaction – destroying all those close to him. He is one of the most odious characters in Hardy's novels. This is not gentle satire, as some critics prefer to see it. Dandies in their carriages on Rotten Row in London are described (in a passage which was rescued from the lost *The Poor Man and the Lady* and gives some idea of its tone) as "occasionally laughing from far down their throats and with their eyes, their mouths not being concerned in the operation at all." Lord Luxellian "somewhat resembled a good-natured commercial traveller of the superior class." Of the superior class! In his earlier novels Hardy often tips his hand in this way: he is not only ironic but caustic.

But social commentary aside, *A Pair of Blue Eyes* contains the ingredients which eventually became expected in any Hardy novel: vivid scenes of Wessex, daring explorations of sexual psychology (although sometimes disguised through a kind of double-language in which he was expert), dramatic incidents in which what passes through the characters' minds is more important than the incidents themselves, and the presence of a "chorus" in the form of rustic characters or bumpkins (there is some self-satire here) who comment on the action from time to time while being unable to influence it.

*A Pair of Blue Eyes* rises above its messy and unresolved story-line in its poetry. It is difficult to discuss how poetry may appear in prose. Pasternak once stated not entirely perversely that "poetry is prose, prose not in the sense of the entirety of all prose works… but prose itself, prose in action… pure prose in its primal intensity." He also stated that prose was life (ie a description of life) but poetry was the "voice of prose". These remarks by another poet who also wrote prose in poetry give some hint toward understanding this phenomenon. In Hardy it often occurs through what reads like a line of a poem, embedded in the prose, as when Stephen remembers Elfride – "How she would wait for him in green places" or in a description of "dreary hills… become black discs vandyked against the sky." But more often it is, to use another of Hardy's title phrases, as a Moment of Vision – an inspired image of the kind which occurs most often in poetry, and which exists in itself, not merely as one more paragraph in a linear narrative. This is why poetry is rare in Hardy's sensation novels, where linear narrative is all important although he will occasionally escape it, as in the dream-like scene in *Desperate Remedies* where Springrove kisses Cytherea while out rowing along the cliffs at Weymouth.

There are several of these dream-like scenes in *A Pair of Blue Eyes*: Knight's ordeal on the cliff-face, Elfride's slipping and being caught by Knight when she is climbing recklessly (like Emma) on a crumbling church tower, a coffin accompanying Stephen and Knight in the same train from London, without their knowing it contains Elfride.

In contrast, there are some clear definitions by Hardy, in his psychological descriptions of Knight, of what it is to be caught in rationality, *not* to be able to think like a poet. "With him, truth seemed too clean and pure an abstraction to be so hopelessly churned in with error as practical persons find it." Knight cannot tolerate ambiguity. He is a prose man. He has "the self respect which had compensated for the lack of self-gratification." But he only comes alive when he faces death, clinging to the more experienced "face" of Beeny cliff while Elfride retreats to make her underwear into a rope. Like Boldwood in *Far from the Madding Crowd*, Knight is so armoured against feeling that feeling destroys his equilibrium: Boldwood, once he is forced to feel, becomes an insane killer. Knight simply relapses into his former moralism which also kills.

Elfride writes dreamy romances, of a poetic kind (shades of Emma's productions in this line), but Knight crushes them in criticism. And she accepts being crushed. Here is Hardy's feminism again – but tempered with realism: Elfride, having been spiritually tyrannised by her empty headed parson father (and by extension by Christianity) has been made incapable of looking after her own interests. She has imagination, but she is also dutiful. She first goes to Stephen to be secretly married but her feelings are overwhelmed – as in those German novels by Kleist and others where the characters are torn between "Pflicht" (duty) and "Gefühl" (feeling) – by her duty to her father. Then she dedicates herself to Knight, who is a suitable match, and goes to him like Ruth ("her prototype", as Hardy remarks, a "bond servant") to Boaz in the Bible, but is crushed by his intellect before he abandons her in prudish horror that she has been previously kissed (by Stephen). Then she is married, dutifully we suppose (her heart is broken) to the newly widowed Lord Luxellian, the commercial traveller type, and is killed in childbirth. Some Romance! But the point is precisely that a romantic girl like Elfride has only one possible fate in Victorian society: to be destroyed by men as even the romantic Emma, to whom he became engaged while writing the novel, might be destroyed by marriage to Hardy himself. Perhaps this personal resonance was too close in time: Hardy had not taken enough distance to be able to write a really good novel about a woman like Elfride. She was too muddled with Emma. Still, like Hardy's later, more robust heroines, although she is a victim she is not entirely passive. Although too crushed by Victorian society to be able to act freely, Hardy's women can certainly think freely – more so, even when uneducated like Tess, than the hidebound or weak men who control them. Quite early in the novel, Elfride is intelligent enough to see her fate: "She thought that the tragedy of her life was beginning."

## *The Trumpet-Major*

*The Trumpet-Major* is set during the Napoleonic Wars, and has a nostalgic, old-fashioned feel, verging on the sentimental. As Wallace Stevens said, "sentiment is a failure of feeling". The marriage, after many tribulations, of the heroine Anne Garland to Bob Loveday (his brother John is the Trumpet Major who also loves Anne but knows she loves Bob better, and so promotes their union: "with the recall of Bob, in which he had been sole agent, his mission seemed to be complete") although sentimentally described leaves an uneasy sense that since Bob, a former sailor, is inherently fickle, it may not work. Hardy explored this kind of outcome unsentimentally, and therefore more movingly, later in *The Woodlanders*, where Grace Melbury is left with the fickle Fitzpiers. Needless to say, this fickleness represents a side of Hardy of which he was well aware: he reduces it finally to the absurd in *The Well-beloved.*

The apparent lightness of *The Trumpet Major* is brought to earth in the final sentence about John's dust in the fields of Spain, which must have the effect on some readers of causing serious reflection on what has seemed so unserious throughout the novel. In fact, when examined closely, the novel reveals a sinister and sordid subtext.

But first, its lightness is a remarkable achievement in itself. The introductory description of Anne is delightful and incidentally shows what could be achieved in the nineteenth century novel, before the cinema speeded up narrative – which had the leisure to *describe*. Anne's complexion is:

> of that particular tint between blonde and brunette which is inconveniently left without a name… the middle point of her upper lip scarcely descending so far as it should have done by rights, so that at the merest pleasant thought, not to mention a smile, portions of two or three white teeth were uncovered whether she would or not. Some people said that this was very attractive… In short, beneath all that was charming and simple in this young woman there lurked a real firmness, unperceived at first, as the speck of colour lurks unperceived in the heart of the palest parsley flower.

Of course "parsley flower" is a give-away – meaning the cow-parsley which grows along every country lane. Just as the "particular tint between blonde and brunette" is not really without a name if the reader considers "mousey." But the description is the reverse of unkind. This is one of

Hardy's greatest strengths: to portray "ordinary" people in their uniqueness, as in fact extraordinary. Anne's rather ordinary prettiness becomes *beauty*. Hardy – again in love with his heroine – is himself like the Loveday brothers and a ridiculous suitor, Festus Derriman, among the "some people" who find such details as a smile which shows "portions of two or three white teeth . . . very attractive."

Cinema could convey none of this. Nor could it include the occasional passages in which the narrative jumps ahead in time to wider contexts than the village behind Weymouth in which most of its action takes place: to the future of the Trumpet Major's regiment in Spain, to the destiny of Bob's ship, which happens to be Nelson's "Victory" on the way to Trafalgar. A film can provide flash-backs, but not "flash-forwards". Although psychologically *The Trumpet Major* is not as profound as Hardy's later novels, it is one of his most masterful in its *mise en scène*. A novelist has simply more scope than that of the film maker.

Anne's courtship by the Loveday brothers is counterpointed by the more plainspun courtship of her mother by their father, Miller Loveday, which presents Anne's probable future in homely detail: in middle-age, married to Miller Bob, she and he will also be stout, slow-moving, stolidly cheerful, and perpetually covered by a fine white dust of flour – unless Bob yields to a fickle impulse, and unprotected by the Trumpet Major who is now a dust more elemental than flour, runs off with some passing actress. He has almost married a London/Weymouth actress, Matilda, who is reminiscent of the actress Eunice in *Desperate Remedies* in that she is a not unsympathetic semi-prostitute. Hardy seems to have liked these women, who may be more than the "stock characters" some critics see them as (after all, economics, snobbish rejection, and circumstance required that many actresses sold themselves to influential men, as Ellen Ternan did to the sanctimonious Dickens), and may represent someone Hardy knew.

*The Trumpet Major* contains a strongly sexual subtext, and not only in its title and the conventional associations of potent soldiers and randy sailors. The buffoonish Festus Derriman who pursues Anne relentlessly almost succeeds in raping her. Even in more simple activities he is described with loving sexual double-entendre: he shakes hands violently, "as if ringing a bell", and the image is masturbatory. All his movements are described as harsh and clumsy, and we know he would be like that if he got Anne to himself. Or if we have any doubt, as usual the name provides the clue. "Derriman" suggests "Dare-he-man", which is harmless enough, but also "Dairyman", which brings in an image of milking on teats, in other words, he is a wanker. And if the reader doubts such sexual innuendoes, the first name "Festus" is surely convincing: most literate Victorians knew enough French to think of "fesse", meaning buttock, and of course the butt of Hardy's humour. (When the American actor Fess Parker featured on billboards in Paris in 1960 or so as Davy Crockett, Fess was changed to "John".) Furthermore, "Festus" suggests "festinate", meaning to hurry, suggesting he would ejaculate prematurely. For Hardy's capacity to indulge in sexual innuendos which both he and his Victorian readers pretended were not present, see the discussion, below, of *Two on a Tower*.

*The Trumpet Major,* although the lightness of tone set in the initial descriptions of Anne and her surroundings survives almost until the end of the novel, is above all an elegy – a sort of Last Post to a vanished epoch in which England fought to the death against a prospective invader, and ordinary people's lives were ennobled. Hardy eventually returned to this, on a self-consciously higher plane, in *The Dynasts*. But there are elegiac passages in *The Trumpet Major* which, in a deliberately humble setting, convey in poetry-in-prose something of what for Hardy was essential to England:

> The present writer, to whom this party has been described times out of number by members of the Loveday family and other aged people now passed away, can never enter the old living-room of Overcombe Mill without beholding the genial scene through the mists of the seventy or eighty years that intervene between then and now. First and brightest to the eye are the dozen candles, scattered about regardless of expense, and kept well snuffed by the miller, who walks round the room at intervals of five minutes, snuffers in hand, and nips each wick with great precision, and with something of an executioner's grim look upon his face as he closes the snuffers upon the neck of the candle. Next to the candle-light show the red and blue coats and white breeches of the soldiers, nearly twenty of them in all besides the ponderous Derriman, the head of the latter, and indeed, the heads of all who are standing up, being in dangerous proximity to the black beams of the ceiling. There is not one among them who would attach any meaning to 'Vittoria', or gather from the syllables 'Waterloo' the remotest idea of his own glory or death...

## *Two on a Tower*

*Two on a Tower* caused something of an outrage when it was published, ostensibly because the heroine, Viviette, makes a marriage of convenience to a Bishop who is persuaded that he is the father of the son to whom she gives birth somewhat prematurely but who is in fact the offspring of her love affair with an aspiring astronomer, Swithin, who is a decade younger than herself. She has also had a depraved husband who was, it seems, eaten by a lion in Africa. The plot is less important in this novel than the sexual relations which were the real reason for the outrage. (Even the Bishop, it is implied, is something of a swine, possibly sexually perverted). In his Forward to later editions Hardy indulged in typical tongue-in-cheek protestations: "There is hardly a single caress in the book outside legal matrimony, or what was intended so to be." Meaning that the love-scenes between Viviette and Swithin, for whom she has adapted an appropriately phallic tower to astronomical observations, mainly occur when they have contracted a secret marriage which is in fact bigamous, since the big-game hunter turns out to have been alive at the time.

Seymour-Smith has pointed out that references to the stars being "well-hung" during the love-scenes evoke a double-meaning known at least back to Shakespeare. But Hardy is naughty, by Victorian standards, throughout. There is a continuing conceit, worthy of Donne, about Swithin's telescope and its probings in the "equatorial" (for the Elizabethans, as Hardy knew, equator equals vagina) that Viviette has given him. And there is blatant punning on "come" in "comet", when the languishing youth, apparently mortally ill, having been kissed by Viviette when asleep (this is before their sexual liaison begins) is then revived by news of a comet: "'O, if I could only live to see that comet through my equatorial!' he cried." Meaning, "if only I could come with you instead of die."

The tense eroticism of *Two on a Tower* is maintained by these double-meanings in the Elizabethan tradition, incongruous though it may seem in a Victorian novel, but also by a more serious poetry-in-prose which, not its rather feeble plot, is what makes this one of Hardy's most moving novels. Many passages can be read as poetry, that is with scrupulous attention to every word: although logically descriptive or expository prose must eliminate ambiguity and "extra" meanings, in poetry words mean everything they mean. For example, the tower is on a "pine-clad protuberance", suggesting a phallus with pubic hair, but also Swithin's "pining" for Viviette within it. And,

> The sob of the environing trees was here expressively manifest... Below the level of their summits the masonry was lichen-stained [ie likin' stained] and mildewed, for the sun [son – Swithin is almost

young enough to be Viviette's son] never pierced that moaning cloud of blue-black vegetation [ie her dark pubic hair]... the pillar rose [ie like a rose] into the sky a bright and cheerful thing, unimpeded, clean and flushed with the sunlight.

Later, as Swithin observes the sun, he is described with a "flush across his cheek". Still later, the spiral staircase to the top of the tower is described as having an "orifice."

When Swithin is sent away by Viviette (the bigamous nature of their marriage has been revealed) to study the stars in South Africa, he reverts to the narcissistic and childish sexuality which she has only temporarily brought him out of, and it is more than hinted that he, contentedly enough, returns to old habits of masturbation: "With a child's simple delight he allowed his instrument to rove, evening after evening..."

To propose that Hardy filled his novels with sexual double-meanings as assiduously as Shakespeare or Ben Jonson did in their plays may seem extreme. But how else, in Victorian England, could this countryman (he even, according to Blunden, had a knack of being able to urinate in the road without stopping walking) convey what he knew to his readers, many of whom also, more or less, knew? He consciously arouses these readers, careful to describe Swithin in all his beauty (to attract female readers), and Viviette in all hers.

But it is a sad novel. Swithin, true to his name (he is constant for 40 days, more or less like the weather after St Swithin's day) ultimately prefers to probe the stars rather than Viviette. He is, as Hardy emphasises with rather heavy irony, more interested in the transit of the heavenly Venus than in the transit of the earthly one Viviette (who is *alive*, as in "*qui vive*", and is also Lady *Constant*ine). She dies of a heart attack in joy at his return. (And if this seems melodramatic, it is nevertheless physiologically accurate: modern research suggests heart attacks often occur in moments of relief after great stress). Swithin, unfazed, will marry a helpmeet sort of girl, Tabitha Lark – a flitting skylark, as it were, with none of Viviette's sexuality. As almost always in his novels (the exceptions are *Far from the Madding Crowd* and *The Mayor of Casterbridge*), Hardy's heroine is a stronger character than any of the males who surround her. But even she is, like Hardy's other "living" heroines (he would describe Emma, when he first knew her as "living"), a victim of male hatred, supported by Christianity, of this so threatening life in women. The novel ends with the phrase: "The Bishop was avenged."

### *The Well-Beloved*

There is something creepy about *The Well-Beloved*. The last published of Hardy's novels, but written before *Jude the Obscure,* it has never caught on except among readers sophisticated in its Shelleyanism, keen to judge it as an extension of his poetry. But his poem of the same name, "The Well-beloved", is as much a think-piece as the novel. What should be exciting about the story of a man who falls in love with three generations of women, all called Avice (A vice?), starting with the grandmother and finishing with the grand-daughter, actually ends up as nauseating. Perhaps this is because it is not apparent that the man, a sculptor called Pierston, actually has sexual relations with any of them. Instead there is another woman, Marcia, a *dea-ex-machina*, whom he marries, abandons, and re-unites with after some 40 years in a Dorian Gray sort of scene (Hardy must have read Wilde's narcissistic little novelette, published in 1890) in which he sees her without her wig and realises that she like him (heavy irony) has aged horribly. (Shades of Augusta Martin, "Amabel"). Pierston (pierce-stone) manages to be infatuated with the three Avices not only without sleeping with them but without expressing his obsession with them in terms of desire. He resembles a scout-master who has crushes on boy-scouts but is too virtuous to admit this is physical. Pierston is pursuing an ideal, or an Ideal, a Platonic form like Shelley who, nevertheless, was robust enough to have carnal relations with his Ideals.

What possessed Hardy to write this? Especially so close to *Jude the Obscure,* in which the protagonist, like Hardy in real life, is very much a victim of his sexual (not idealistic) urges. Perhaps *The Well-Beloved* is a sort of residue of *Jude*, an exorcism of an unhealthy tendency in its author. Autobiographically, it is interesting. As Pierston says in a *cri de coeur*, "When was it to end, this course of his heart not ageing while his frame moved naturally onward? Perhaps only with life." This echoes the poem about "this fragile frame at eve / Shaken with sobbings of noontide", but there is a subtle double-entendre: the "course" may end not, as cliché would dictate, with death, but "with life" – perhaps a new love, before death.

Although classed among Romances and Fantasies, *The Well-Beloved* is in its own way a novel of ingenuity. Having resolved, as a young man, to live life "as emotion", here is Hardy pursuing the idea to its extreme: a life lived "as emotion" but without anything else. This requires an ingenious playing with reality. Instead of, as he might have if more literal-minded, simply telling the story of his infatuation for the three Sparks sisters, or whatever other series of women he had in mind, Hardy must invent a situation in which his hero can contrive to be engaged to be married to three generations of Avices. He must thereby invent a society which fits this fantasy. He locates it on Portland Bill, off Weymouth, known formerly as the Isle of Slingers, and supposedly inhabited by the descendants of Roman sailors. The Avices share the surname Caro, which is vaguely Italianate as well as being the home of "Island Custom", a form of trial marriage, of which Pierston does not, in fact, take advantage. At the one moment when he might have been ready to do so, when he has arranged to elope with Avice I, she does not turn up: "Had she appeared, the primitive betrothal, with its natural result, would probably have taken place; and, as no islander [Pierston is an islander too] had ever been known to break that compact, she would have become his wife." *The Well-Beloved* is not (unlike most of Hardy's novels) about sex, but about the emotion which swirls around sex – in this case artificially divorced from it.

To complicate matters, Pierston is himself related to the three Avices. Apart from giving an artificial frisson of incest (à la Shelley), this introduces the theme of heredity: Pierston's obsessive fickleness is more than matched by his Avices, though not always negatively. Pierston is "fickle lover in the brief, faithful friend in the long term", as the Avices are, each in her turn, to him. Hardy cared deeply for friendship between men and women: he remained friends for decades with Florence Henniker and Agnes Grove, even after they had rejected his attempts to seduce them (unfortunately, seduction was one of only three accepted styles for the beginning of a sexual relationship among the Victorians, the others being financial purchase and rape), and, touchingly, at the age of 84 he followed his last love, Gertrude Bugler, out to an awaiting car in order to tell her, "If anyone asks you if you knew Thomas Hardy, say yes, he was your friend." But in *The Well-Beloved*, friendship seems manipulated in comparison with what we know of Hardy's life. This is a novel which, splitting off a portion of its creator, becomes not larger than life, but smaller.

The problem is that having cut out (uncharacteristically) the flesh "It was not the flesh; he had never knelt low to that" Hardy was left with only the fussy dramas of possession. And this displaces his real theme, of friendship replacing carnal love between man and woman, in "cordial loving kindness." But, given the realities Hardy is courageously willing to confront in his other novels, this is a doomed project. No wonder, at the end of the novel, Pierston's "life seemed... a ghost story." As Marcia (who has unrealistically disappeared from the action for almost forty years but who emerges in somewhat the same pickle as Pierston) puts it, she is "an old friendless woman... and you an old friendless man."

Yet none of Hardy's think-pieces, in verse or prose, is entirely without poetry, and *The Well-Beloved* provides memorable images of Portland. In a place Hardy calls Deadman's Bay, "there arose a deep, hollow stroke like the single beat of a drum, the intervals being filled with a long-drawn rattling, as of bones between huge canine jaws." This was a place of the drowned "who had rolled each other to oneness on that restless sea-bed."

# 5 Novels of Character and Circumstance: 1

## *Under the Greenwood Tree* (1872), *Far from the Madding Crowd* (1874), *The Return of the Native* (1878)

### *Under the Greenwood Tree*

Hardy in his Preface to *Under the Greenwood Tree,* for the Wessex edition, described it as a "story of the Mellstock Quire and its old established west-gallery musicians", as if the romance between Dick Dewy and Fancy Day (the names bespeaking innocence and Springtime) was not important to him – and probably it was not, apart from its function of pumping the reader's sentiment (that failure of feeling). Subtitled "A Rural Painting of the Dutch School", this second of Hardy's published novels, written at home at Bockhampton in an interval of his engagement to Emma, seems a cynical exercise: this "rural painting" has nothing in common with those Breughel pictures where bulging peasants fornicate drunkenly behind tables as they undoubtedly did at the parties for which Hardy as a boy violinist, his father and the original members of the Mellstock (ie Stinsford) Quire did the honours. As Geoffrey Grigson (for once a poet writing the Introduction to a Hardy novel) points out, it was in Hardy's interest, about to marry the niece of an Archdeacon after all, and having written the sensationalist *Desperate Remedies*, to write something respectable. *Under the Greenwood Tree* is the first of Hardy's novels to present the pastoral world which became known as "Wessex". *Desperate Remedies* had in fact been just as much set in this world, but not so self-consciously. Hardy's sub-title tips us off: this novel is a fake. A necessary one, however. The pastoral world it defines becomes the world of the much more daring novels which would follow and promote what critics would describe as "Wessexmania" a discreet Victorian allusion to "sexmania."

A main ingredient of this pastoral world is the "rustic chorus" of peasant characters making their commentary on the action, but as Grigson points out, "the way Hardy presents his peasant types. . . distresses the modern reader. They are patronized. They are not the peasants of Breughel… They are yokels… 'stunpoles' or blockheads." In the *Life,* Hardy admits that "he had rather burlesqued them."

This novel achieved its end. It cornered a sentimental readership whose failure in feeling would be replaced by an education in feeling in subsequent novels in the same genre – though to classify it as a novel of Character and Circumstance is pushing it. The romance between the simple tranter (carter) Dick Dewy and the not quite so simple village schoolteacher Fanny pursues its predestined end with only one hitch: Fanny is somewhat attracted to the young vicar, Mr Maybold, as much a loser as the similarly named Boldwood in *Far from the Madding Crowd*, but a stuffed shirt of superior status to the girl he wants to marry, or more accurately possess. In Hardy's "rural painting" the tints are subtle, but Maybold is no less obnoxious and hypocritical than any of Hardy's clergymen. And, as critics eager to redeem this novel from slightness have pointed out, Fanny marries Dick with some hint of regret for his not being Maybold: she is doomed to a life of obscurity instead of semi-obscurity, and the modicum of education she has received to become a schoolteacher will go to waste. These are themes which Hardy will address more forcefully in later novels of character and circumstance. The bittersweet undertone of Fancy's marriage to Dick is taken up again in *Far from the Madding Crowd* where Bathsheba Everdene has to settle for the trusty Gabriel Oak instead of the glamorous Troy or the crazed but gentlemanly Boldwood, and the reverse situation is explored in *The Woodlanders* where Grace Melbury is dissuaded by her ambitious father from marrying the trusty Giles Winterbourne and ends up with the intelligent but unreliable Fitzpiers. Hardy, perhaps from his experience of Tryphena Sparks and his sister Mary going into schoolteaching, was sympathetic to the ambitions of young women to better themselves. Put simply (although this is not the language of political correctness) Dick is less bright than Fancy, and this is in its own way tragic.

So *Under the Greenwood Tree* is slightly spoiled, although Dick Dewy is a decent man, by the picture of Fanny being led to marriage like a beast to the slaughter. But, as Hardy's later Preface reveals, this was less interesting to him than what the novel is really about: the vanishing world of rural Wessex. He could never forgive the new parson at Stinsford who in the 1830s dismissed the Quire, the band of local players, including Thomas Hardy Senior, who sat in the gallery and who might even make their own instruments, and certainly kept their own collections of music scrawled out in old notebooks which, in the words of Hardy's friend Hermann Lea, often contained "a curious mixture of carols, secular songs, psalms, and quaint ditties more suitable to Christmas revelry than church worship." These Quires were replaced by the latest in pump organs, played by a respectable young lady as Emma played the organ at St Juliot: was *Under the Greenwood Tree* a half-conscious protest by Hardy at what he was committing himself to?

At worst the novel is unbearably twee: "If ever a woman looked a divinity Fancy Day appeared one that morning as she floated down those school steps, in the form of a nebulous collection of colours inclining to blue." Or, as Grigson points out, squirmingly patronising:

> "And who's that young man?" the vicar said.
> "Tell the pa'son yer name," said the tranter, turning to Leaf, who stood with his elbows nailed back to a bookcase.
> "Please, Thomas Leaf, your holiness!" said Leaf, trembling.

But at best it creates a landscape (not, pretentiously, of the Dutch school, but simply of Hardy's own), as in the very first paragraph:

> To dwellers in a wood almost every species of tree has its voice as well as its feature. At the passing of the breeze the fir-trees sob and moan less distinctly than they rock; the holly whistles as it battles with itself; the ash hisses amid its quiverings; the beech rustles while its flat boughs rise and fall…

And even the rustic chorus scenes can take on a macabre, authentic life –

> "Ah, Sam was a man," said Mr Penny contemplatively.
> "Sam was!" said Bowman.
> "Especially for a drap o' drink," said the tranter.
> "Good, but not religious-good", suggested Mr Penny.
> The tranter nodded. Having at last made the tap and hole quite ready, "Now then, Suze, bring a mug," he said. "Here's luck to us, my sonnies!"

enough to merit being lifted, without acknowledgement, by the American poet e. e. cummings ("Sam was a man…").

Much as one may despise the sentimentality of *Under the Greenwood Tree*, its image of a lost rural England remains in the mind. And it fulfilled its purpose by hooking a readership, thus revealing Hardy as, at bottom, utterly *un*sentimental. He simply knew that most readers (then as now, when readers head for their summer holidays primed with safe novels from the lists published in the Sunday papers) first of all want to encounter what they already know, or think they know – for example, that the countryside is a pretty place full of charming yokels, which makes one think complacently of olde England. It takes time to lead them into more frightening and unexpected terrain. Hardy, once he had his readership, took that time.

## *Far from the Madding Crowd*

The title of *Far from the Madding Crowd* is taken from Gray's Elegy ("Far from the madding crowd's ignoble strife") but ironically, of course, since the heroine Bathsheba, once she comes into possession of her father's farm and decides to manage it for herself, is surrounded and "madded" by much ignoble strife among her suitors.

Almost all Hardy's novels (the exceptions being the novels of ingenuity, which are self-consciously contemporary) are set in a time some decades before his present. This creates a distancing effect, so that the novel becomes almost mythical.

*Far from the Madding Crowd* is a pastoral, like *Under the Greenwood Tree*, but brought out into the windswept openness of sheep-farmed downlands, where a more glaring light does not allow the mellow sentiment of "the Dutch school" and its interiors of cottages and sheltered woodland paths. Even the sheep are not dotted picturesquely over the landscape, but have a hard life of births leading to ewes' deaths and, in the case of Gabriel Oak's flock, being herded by an errant dog over the edge of a cliff.

The names of characters accentuate the mythical effect. Gabriel is a "good shepherd", and a protecting angel. Bathsheba evokes the Bible and David's love for a goddess-like figure seen bathing. Sergeant Troy evokes the heroic Iliad, with the acknowledgement that this sword-wielding soldier has a passive streak and through his impressive beauty brings women to lay siege to him: who is really seducing whom? Some of Hardy's characterisation in this novel suggests types developed in 20th century psychoanalysis. Troy is the narcissistic character par excellence. One of his rivals, Boldwood (his name suggesting his English robustness, but his emotional woodenness and deadness in contrast to Gabriel who is a kind of living tree), is a typical obsessive-compulsive, locked in what Freud called a "neurotic equilibrium", and Reich described as "character armour." Hardy's description of him could belong, though better written, in a Reichian textbook:

> That stillness, which struck casual observers more than anything else in his character and habit, and seemed so precisely like the rest of inanition, may have been the perfect balance of enormous antagonistic forces – positives and negatives in fine adjustment. His equilibrium disturbed, he was in extremity at once. If an emotion possessed him at all, it ruled him; a feeling not mastering him was entirely latent.

This brilliance of characterisation sometimes deserted Hardy (it is far from evident in his penultimate novel, *The Well-Beloved)*, but *Far from the Madding Crowd* shows that he was capable of it from 1874, at least. It applies even to the novel's minor figures, and at lighter moments. One of Hardy's rustic chorus characters describes how Bathsheba's father, a tailor (a traditionally lecherous profession) used to liven up his marriage:

> The poor feller was faithful and true enough to her in his wish, but his heart would rove, do what he would... But at last I believe he cured it by making her take off her wedding-ring and calling her by her maiden name as they sat together after the shop was shut, and so 'a would get to fancy she was only his sweetheart, and not married to him at all. And as soon as he could thoroughly fancy he was doing wrong and committing the seventh, 'a got to like her as well as ever, and they lived on a perfect picture of mutel love.

So Hardy, aware of being chronically fickle himself, and on the point of marrying Emma, may have consoled himself with hopeful thoughts of the future. But this is typically "mischievous": he is ever-so-amusingly but quite dangerously dissecting the anatomy of lust within marriage, tipping his hat to the role of imagination in sex, and cocking a snook at the (Pauline) Christian view – that sex is all right within marriage so long as it is not done for its own sake – by turning this view on its head. The husband is "at last" (ie previously he has in reality been adulterous) able to save his marriage by pretending he is "doing wrong and committing the seventh" (ie breaking the seventh commandment, against adultery). Hardy only just wriggles out of the possibility of Christian censure by his humorous emphasis on the "fancy" dedicated to what is technically a moral end, the preservation of a marriage.

This passage slipped past Hardy's friend Leslie Stephen (father of Virginia Woolf) who provided him with editorial advice, which he followed, though grudgingly, in his early novels, about what was acceptable to readers.

But *Far from the Madding Crowd* could have been an even more daring book. For example, Hardy's original manuscript of the scene where Bathsheba breaks open Fanny Robin's coffin and finds as she expects that it also contains the body of a stillborn child, fathered by Troy, contained a description of the baby's body, "having the soft convexity of mushrooms on a dewy morning", but all description of the baby was left out on Stephen's advice. There were also many small alterations which shift the book towards respectability: for example, again on Stephen's advice, the word "buttocks" was changed to "backs" in a description of sheep!

*Far from the Madding Crowd* is a moving book, in its overt description of emotion, by a writer who seems to have felt what he describes: "Directly he had gone, Bathsheba burst into great sobs, dry-eyed sobs, which cut as they came, without any softening by tears." It is also moving in its covert suggestion of emotional torment in the stoical Gabriel and the rigid Boldwood and, paradoxically in its acknowledgement of the fickle Troy's lack of emotion, which, after all, leads to painful emotional consequences to those around him. He is, indeed, something of a psychopath: he "had a power of eluding grief by simply adjourning it", and "what Troy had in the way of emotion was the occasional fitful sentiment."

Then why does Bathsheba – why do women?, 'respectable men' might ask – fall in love with a psychopath like Troy? This is not, and probably cannot be explained. But on the evidence that Hardy seems aware of, on the one hand Bathsheba is quite simply attracted to his animal spirits and virility, and on the other she is as surely as even dear little Fancy Day with her crush on the handsome young clergyman from a different class aware that marriage to the loyal and solid Gabriel Oak, though not as dire as marriage to the muscle-bound Boldwood, is going to be a little on the dull side: *sexually*. Her being used by the fickle Troy – fucked and abandoned, to put it simply – teaches her a lesson. Whether this has been paid for by a loss of sexual desire is not made completely clear. The implication has been that, as her father's daughter (Hardy believed grimly in heredity) Bathsheba herself might well be capable of "fancy" to commit "the seventh". Her impulsive marriage to Troy is due, after all, to the absolute necessity that they should make love and although the novel states that this occurs after the marriage, room is left for the possibility that it occurs before.

Much is made, in the marriage of Bathsheba and Gabriel which ends the book, of how unromantic it is, and how it consists largely of "good-fellowship" and "camaraderie". The only consolation for romantics is that these qualities are described as "superadded to love between the sexes." And there is no doubt that Gabriel, who is after all no angel but a man of the soil, will take pleasurable and lusty advantage of his possession: "Oh – Oh!" said Gabriel, with a low laugh of joyousness. 'My own dear…' " But where Bathsheba finds herself sexually is not expressed. And the implication is that it cannot be – either by her, as a fictional character, or by Hardy himself. In a key phrase in the novel, Hardy, although no feminist in the narrow political sense, puts his finger on the issue which had already preoccupied him in *Desperate Remedies* and *The Hand of Ethelberta* (the early Hardy, of these novels and of *Far from the Madding Crowd*, was as radical as the later one): in reply to Boldwood's nagging and typically male request to Bathsheba to state exactly what she feels about him, she replies:

> I don't know – at least, I cannot tell you. It is difficult for a woman to define her feelings in language which is chiefly made by men to express theirs.

### *Under the Greenwood Tree*

If *Under the Greenwood Tree* is a straight pastoral, and *Far from the Madding Crowd* an ironic pastoral, *The Return of the Native* is an anti-pastoral. The woods and downs are replaced by a blasted heath and indeed the scene is *Macbeth*-like, with the heroine, or anti-heroine, Eustacia Vye like a witch, accompanied by her male witch former and future lover Damon (daimon, demon) Wildeve (wild evening). Eustacia means "steadfast" in Greek, and Vye suggesting trying (vying) for a prize: she is supposedly of Corfiote-Greek origin, though she has grown up in Weymouth with an English father, and she hates and is bored by Egdon heath where she has been brought to live, and which she prowls incessantly by day and night having become, paradoxically, its creature, her ancient Mediterranean nature (Victorian anthropology was crude, but this is Hardy's drift) appropriate to its ancient inhabitants of Mediterranean origin who left their prehistoric monument, the Rainbarrow, which she haunts. Her entrances and exits might as well be accompanied by claps of thunder, and her declamations are histrionic. Her final exit is into a millrace where she is drowned clutched in a love-death struggle with Wildeve, but before that she has chewed up and spat out the hapless hero, Clym Yeobright, who aspires after calm (Clym = clement) and is something of a seer (Yeobright suggests Eyebright, the herb that promotes clear seeing), but who ends the novel blind, and as a preacher stomping the heath and surrounding towns telling his story. The blindness suggests an Oedipus theme, and in fact Clym is the native who has returned to the heath after foreign travel, to his mother, Mrs Yeobright: they are as "close as two hands", which critics have not been slow to see as a hint at Hardy and his mother, Jemima Hand, who is undoubtedly the woman described in the poem 'Ex Tenebris': "She who upheld me, and I, in the midmost of Egdon together."

The suggestion, at the subtext level which is unusually dominant in this novel, is that Clym is drawn back to the heath and the security of his mother, but in so far as he is a sexual being (not very passionately, which seems to be why Eustacia returns to her Damon) the woman of the heath with whom he must have congress, and who inevitably destroys him, is its female spirit or demoness, Eustacia. She is mainly a creature of the night. The imagery of the novel is of changing light and dark, even down to the famous scene in which the reddleman Diggory Venn plays cards with Wildeve for high stakes – money in gold guineas which belongs to Clym's cousin Thomasin, who has disastrously married Wildeve, but whom Venn protects – in pitch darkness by the light of fireflies. But once Clym has married Eustacia, after pledging himself to her on the Rainbarrow at an eclipse of the moon, he must work on the heath to support her, his eyesight having failed after long and inappropriate study, so that he cannot realise her dreams of taking her out of Egdon and to Paris. He is in effect turned into an armoured, insect-like creature and burned up by the unremitting sun (described elsewhere as a "merciless incendiary") as he cuts furze (from the furze or gorse plants which have golden flowers and which Hardy may well have known were in Celtic myth associated with the sun):

> This man from Paris was now so disguised by his leather accoutrements, and by the goggles he was obliged to wear over his eyes, that his closest friend might have passed by without recognizing him. He was a brown spot in the midst of an expanse of olive-green gorse, and nothing more... His daily life was of a curious microscopic sort, his whole world being limited to a circuit of a few feet from his person. His familiars were creeping and winged things, and they seemed to enroll him in their band. Bees hummed around his ears with an intimate air, and tugged at the heath and the furze-flowers at his side in such numbers as to weight them down to the sod. The strange amber-coloured butterflies which Egdon produced, and which were never seen elsewhere, quivered in the breath of his

> lips, alighted on his bowed back, and sported with the glittering point of his hook as he flourished it up and down.

And as Clym toils like this, he sings a ditty in French, called "Le point du jour." Perhaps some of the emotional drive for this novel came from a horror in Hardy of ever returning to the "microscopic" world of his native Dorset: in 1878, he had not yet made that decision. Whatever its origins, this dense poetic prose forms much of *The Return of the Native.* The poetry is not only in its intensely vivid and minutely observant description of the heath, but in its reflecting back and forth the obsessive emotional imagery of the story: here the (golden) gorse flowers, the (golden) bees, the (golden) amber-coloured butterflies, all of which express the sun (like Montale's "girasole impazzito di luce", "sunflower maddened by light") which is burning Clym up as he descends into darkness, reduced from civilised man to something approaching an insect – yet strangely not unhappy: "when in the full swing of labour he was cheerfully disposed and calm."

Mrs Yeobright, alienated by her son's marriage, has a heart attack while resting on a bed of thyme during a long trek to attempt a reconciliation with him, and he finds her in time to be with her at her death. The spirits of the heath, in the form of a would-be witch, of the Anglo-Saxon sort, Susan Nunsuch, who burns a wax effigy of Eustacia, have their revenge in Eustacia's drowning with Wildeve. Clym takes up preaching. And Thomasin, Clym's sweet cousin whom Wildeve has seduced, married, and now widowed, although Mrs Yeobright would have wanted her to marry Clym, is rescued by the mysterious reddle-man, Diggory Venn, who has disappeared from the heath but now returns to claim her in marriage: the novel ends on this light and upbeat note.

Hardy wrote in a footnote to the 1912 edition:

> The writer may state here that the original conception of the story did not design a marriage between Thomasin and Venn. He was to have retained his isolated and weird character to the last, and to have disappeared mysteriously from the heath, nobody knowing whither, Thomasin remaining a widow. But certain circumstances of serial publication led to a change of interest.
> Readers can therefore choose between the endings, and those with an austere artistic code can assume the more consistent conclusion to be the true one.

It is assumed by critics that "the more consistent conclusion" is Venn's disappearance. Some critics, eg Millgate, claim that here Hardy's judgement was at fault: that the ending as published is appropriate to most readers. Others, eg Seymour-Smith, indignantly opt for the more gloomy ending as poetically, and realistically, preferable. But it could be that Hardy was divided within himself: it would be quite like him to raise the possibility of the alternative ending because of a fundamental and unresolvable ambivalence in his own feelings. The phrase "the more consistent conclusion" may be tongue in cheek. Consistent with what? It is the reader's choice. In effect, the 1912 footnote is a device worthy of the 20th century modernism soon to come: the reader is actually being given a choice of endings!

Whether or not it is consistent, Thomasin's marriage to Venn is touching and has its own poetry. After all, he has disappeared, and now appears as if he is magical, which he is as the only person in the novel, though presumably illiterate, and certainly devoid of high ideas, who really sees clearly, and all his actions are deft, moral, and sensitive. He is a sort of white witch, among so many black or at least dark ones. Venn (as Hardy probably knew from his conversations about Celtic and Anglo-Saxon etymology with William Barnes) is the Welsh, and ancient British, word for "white." Or, most accurately he is a red witch: he is blood-red from the reddle, the red dye with which, as part of his trade, he marks sheep. Eustacia is a black witch dedicated to the moon and its eclipses, as in *Macbeth* and ancient Greece. Venn is dedicated to the sun, and represents it, at last, as a creative, not a destructive agent.

Much in *The Return of the Native* is melodramatic, some of the characterisation is weak (notably, as Seymour-Smith points out, that of Wildeve, who in an early manuscript of the novel is a more interesting witch-like figure called Toogood), and Eustacia's histrionics and Mediterranean sensuality are easily dismissed conventional clichés. But modern psychopathology sees fit to define a "histrionic" personality disorder, as a politically correct substitute for the former "hysteric." Both labels are defensive psychiatrist-speak for "sexually expressive". There are, in fact, many women like Eustacia: she is compelling in her demands for a sexual and emotional satisfaction which she has no chance of achieving in the world in which she finds herself.

As is widely acknowledged, the heath itself is the most powerful character in the story. And the characters themselves are less important, perhaps, than the dynamic tensions between them, which drive the poetry in the prose. True, Eustacia and Clym are not fully "realised", and Eustacia in particular does not "develop". *The Return of the Native* would probably not nowadays satisfy a publisher's reader that it contains a well worked out plot. However, once read it is unforgettable.

# 6 Novels of Character and Circumstance: 2

## *The Mayor of Casterbridge* (1886)
## *The Woodlanders* (1887)
## *Tess of the Durbervilles* (1891)
## *Jude the Obscure* (1895)

### *The Mayor of Casterbridge*

As *Tess* does with its eponymous heroine, so *The Mayor* does with its eponymous (anti-)hero, who develops, changes, struggles, and is ultimately defeated at the hands of the Fates. Tess, as a woman, is mainly a victim of circumstance. Similarly Grace, the not-quite heroine but certainly the central character of *The Woodlanders*. But the Mayor, Michael Henchard, being a man, is in Hardy's scheme of things, like Jude in *Jude the Obscure*, more actively responsible for his destiny. It is as if, in the final four Novels of Character and Circumstance, Hardy is putting his cards on the table and stating a view that for men character equals destiny (with circumstance throwing in its usual hostile or indifferent twists), but for women circumstance equals destiny (with character throwing in its usual dispositions to weakness and error).

This is a sort of Wessex *King Lear*, with Henchard starting earlier than Lear, as a poor, hard-drinking hay-trusser who makes the mistake (or it may be, ironically, a good move) of selling his wife and baby daughter, Elizabeth-Jane, when drunk on furmity (an ancient drink of fermented grains, sold by a witch-like "furmity woman"), at auction. She is bought by a passing sailor, and when Henchard awakes next morning he forswears drink and moves to Casterbridge where he makes a success of a grain business (furmity in another form) and becomes Mayor. Eventually the sold wife, her sailor having died, turns up in Casterbridge with her daughter Elizabeth-Jane (by the sailor but Henchard thinks she is the original Elizabeth-Jane, who has in fact died) and Henchard, after a meeting in an ancient British earthwork, marries her again, for form's sake. After various twists and turns, Henchard is displaced in his grain business by a Scot, Donald Farfrae, whom he has encouraged, and who marries Henchard's former girlfriend, the blatantly sensual (and therefore not wholly English: she comes from Jersey) Lucetta. Henchard takes to drink again (his twenty year vow is up), becomes a recluse, is cared for, then rejected because of false information, by his Cordelia-like supposed daughter Elizabeth-Jane, and finally wanders off across Dorset to die in isolation after which, when Lucetta has died of a miscarriage, having been mocked in effigy as Henchard's whore in a "skimmity ride" parade through Casterbridge, Elizabeth-Jane marries the efficient but sentimental and essentially cool-hearted Farfrae, who is scientific about grain (he has a mysterious method of making bad grain seem good), not a helpless corn-god victim of it like Henchard.

At the end Henchard knows that even the daughter he loved is not his own. (He is also without issue: his seed, his grain, has come to nothing). He leaves, scrawled in pencil on "a crumpled scrap of paper",

> MICHAEL HENCHARD'S WILL
> That Elizabeth-Jane Farfrae be not told of my death, or made to grieve on account of me.
> & that I be not bury'd in consecrated ground.
> & that no sexton be asked to toll the bell.
> & that nobody is wished to see my dead body.
> & that no murners walk behind me at my funeral.
> & that no flours be planted on my grave.
> & that no man remember me.
> To this I put my name.
> Michael Henchard

Elizabeth-Jane, when she reads these words knows that "the man who wrote them meant what he said." This is a key line, since it contrasts Henchard with her own new husband, who while decent and law-abiding is also rigidly proper, and is capable of singing sentimental ditties about Scotland without actually feeling them or acting on them (by going home, for example). Farfrae is not only "far frae" his native land, he is "far frae" his deep feelings. Henchard is Dorset through and through, and although his behaviour is mainly bad, and includes cruelty, lying and deception (although he has also been decent enough to try and prevent the skimmity ride), he is always aware of what he thinks and feels. He creeps away from Casterbridge, dressed in his old hay-trusser clothes, heading Eastwards for six days, until he is far from home and stops to die in a deserted hut with only a simpleton farmboy (cf. the Fool in *Lear*) to care for him.

On the Sunday on which he has resumed drinking, he has insisted, with threatening oaths, that the church (instrumental) "choir", who have repaired to the Three Mariners Inn after the morning service, should play the 109th psalm to the setting "Wiltshire": "old Wiltshire is the only tune worth singing, the psalm tune that would make my blood ebb and flow like the sea when I was a steady chap."

He recites the versified psalm, which ends

> A swift destruction soon shall seize
>   On his unhappy race;
> And the next age his hated name
>   Shall utterly deface.

Readers interested in music could do well to look up "Wiltshire" in the Church of England Hymnal: the tune dips down a semi-tone in the end word of each phrase, with a finalising and infinitely sad effect.

Although Henchard can be said to "develop", because his behaviours change, and he follows his tragic ascent and decline, Hardy makes it clear that he does not believe that Henchard, or anyone else, truly changes in character, although the shallow Farfrae thinks so:

> Henchard, a poor man in his employ, was not, to Farfrae's view, the Henchard who had ruled him. Yet he was not only the same man, but that man, with his sinister qualities, formerly latent, quickened into life by his buffetings.

Farfrae, who "duly" kisses Lucetta from time to time, and is an ideal husband, does not know that she has been, at one stage, Henchard's mistress, and that she has enjoyed this. (Although not stated in so many words, Hardy makes this amply clear). And Henchard has been a hard task master in business. As one of his former workers, the simpleton Abel Whittle, who has been taken over with the business by Farfrae, says, "tis better for us than 'twas… We work harder, but we bain't made afeard now." But "'tis a shilling a week less."

Farfrae is a foil for Henchard. And none of the three female characters in the novel – the sold wife, Susan, the rather constrained but thoughtful Elizabeth-Jane, and the reckless Lucetta is strong enough to draw great attention. Uniquely, in Hardy's novels, this is a story in which the main protagonists are men. Farfrae and Henchard are versions of a virtuous / wicked pair of male alter egos which is met in Springrove / Manston, Somerset / Dare, Angel / Alex, Oak / Troy, Winterbourne / Fitzpiers. In the earlier novels, the contrast between virtuous and wicked is as between white and black. But as the novels proceed, it becomes more subtle. Alex, admittedly, in *Tess*, represents a partial slide back to a Manston type stage villain. But, like the other great seducer, Sergeant Troy, he has at least fleeting moments of feeling – though provoked by guilt. Fitzpiers, in *The Woodlanders*, is also a seducer, but not a caricature villain: he is capable of love, only incapable of resisting lust, and he is a skilled though not always caring doctor. Since Henchard is so pre-eminent in *The Mayor of Casterbridge,* it is easy to miss his function in a pair with Farfrae (who, like Hardy's other virtuous male characters is lacking in sexual drive), and thus his function as villain of the piece. But he *is*, by the usual standards, a villain. It is one of Hardy's most extraordinary achievements that most readers end the novel liking him in spite of his (unwhitewashed) wickedness.

As Seymour-Smith, ever close to Hardy's inner motives, points out, Henchard (the name, even, echoes Hardy) may be in part a projection of Hardy's fears that in his planned move to Dorchester (which equals Casterbridge in his "Wessex"), which Emma might come to regret (as she in fact did), he was pursuing his ends as ruthlessly as Henchard. He also seems to have had at least fantasies, in his darker moments, of getting rid of Emma. Not that he would have. But the novels of a poet, unlike more usual novels by glorified journalists, may contain many such projections: not unconscious ones, as Freudians would suppose, but painfully conscious ones – hence their power, which derives largely from honesty.

But in the end even the male-centred *The Mayor of Casterbridge* turns at last to the fate of a woman. The thoughtful Elizabeth-Jane finds herself "in a latitude of calm weather" in which she has come through to wisdom:

> As the lively and sparkling emotions of her early married life cohered into an equable serenity, the finer movements of her nature found scope in discovering to the narrow-lived ones around her the secret (as she had once learnt it) of making limited opportunities endurable; which she deemed to consist in the cunning enlargement, by a species of microscopic treatment, of those minute forms of satisfaction that offer themselves to everybody not in positive pain.

Similarly, after all, even Clym Yeobright as he toiled like an insect, "microscopic" on the heath, was "cheerfully disposed and calm." This quiet but carefully written conclusion to *The Mayor of Casterbridge* ends with the sentence:

> And in being forced to class herself among the fortunate she did not cease to wonder at the persistence of the unforseseen, when the one

> to whom such unbroken tranquillity had been accorded in the adult stage was she whose youth had seemed to teach that happiness was but the occasional episode in a general drama of pain.

Just as in the lines in "Ex Tenebris" (see Chapter 7) about how he "upgathered and cast forth the snow from the crocus border", Hardy slips into a general conclusion of gloom a telling line of hope. Through Elizabeth-Jane (and these names may have been dear to him: think of Elizabeth and Jane Nicholls), he is wondering at the possible existence of a law of nature (probably the same one that the biologist Paul Kammerer would propose to explain the series of interconnected events which emerged from nature's inherent "Beharrung", meaning persistence) which opens the possibility that even for a person who realistically, if gloomily, expects the worst, wonderful things may happen, in "the persistence of the unforeseen."

## *The Woodlanders*

*The Woodlanders* was Hardy's favourite among his novels. It is the most quintessentially animistic, its title the only one which refers not to a theme or a particular person, but to a community, set like a clock to the necessities of the natural round. It is troubled by the return of the heroine Grace Melbury from an education insisted on by her ambitious timber-merchant father, which has given her civilised ideas and leads her to doubt her old love for the woodsman Giles Winterbourne. Thus primed, she falls for the fickle attentions of an outsider, the doctor, Edred Fitzpiers, who is in effect over-educated: when not practising a rather theoretical kind of medicine, he is immersed in philosophical literature. After marrying Grace, who rejects Giles, Fitzpiers abandons her for Felice Charmond, also an outsider, an older woman (who wears a hair piece which has originated, via a hairdresser who has bought it, in the hair of Marty South, who is fruitlessly in love with Giles) with whom he runs away to a high life on the Continent (as Clym Yeobright should have done with Eustacia Vye, whom the dramatic and sensual Felice resembles). Felice has nursed Fitzpiers after he has been beaten up, after a fall from his horse, by Grace's father, Melbury, enraged by his attachment to Felice. Before this, Fitzpiers has been attempting to treat Marty South's father, who is obsessively convinced that the elm tree outside his cottage window will fall on him and kill him: Fitzpiers's scientific prescription is the felling of the elm tree but when South sees it is gone he instantly dies. When Fitzpiers eventually returns to the woodlands (after a row with Felice because he has discovered that her hair is partly false and after, providentially, Felice has been gunned down by a jilted American ex-lover) to reclaim Grace, he finds she has become close to Giles again. She runs away to Giles, who has been impoverished by Felice's off-hand reclaiming of a leasehold, and finds him where he is working in the woods: decently, he puts her up in his hut but is too proper to share it with her. In the rain, he sleeps nearby in the woods, and becomes ill with typhoid fever. (Although this follows no medical description of the disease it is explained away by the supposition that it must have been lying dormant in Giles). Although nursed by Grace, he dies. Fitzpiers, who arrives late on the scene, tries to save Giles but cannot, and now, repentant, he has Grace to himself. Their love is rekindled after she narrowly escapes being maimed in a man-trap set for Fitzpiers by a young villager, Timothy Tangs, who has discovered that his new wife, Suke Damson, has been Fitzpiers's mistress. (Setting the trap is Timothy's last act before he and Suke emigrate to Australia and a new life.) Marty South is left to tend the grave of Giles, possessing him at last.

This is, no doubt, a fantastic plot – as if Hardy, after the noble simplicity of *The Mayor of Casterbridge* has returned to the mad convolutions of his earlier Novels of Ingenuity. But, although stretched to the limit, the plot serves its purpose: it is a framework for an intensely realised series of images, almost poems, through which the novels' characters work out, and become aware of, their destiny. *The Woodlanders* shows that a novel by a poet does not need to have a plot in the ordinary prose sense: it is the poetic sense that counts. So Giles dies of love for Grace: the nature of his fever is an irrelevance. So the old woodlander South's very life is bound up with an elm tree in ways that he, and certainly a scientific doctor, cannot understand. And so Marty and Giles cling to each other asexually like trees.

Hardy wrote a poem about trees, "In a Wood" (erroneously retitled "From *The Woodlanders*") in the year the novel appeared, in which they appear as

> Combatants all!
> Sycamore shoulders oak,
> Vines the slim sapling yoke,
> Ivy-spun halters choke
> Elms stout and tall.

And in the novel he wrote:

> The leaf was deformed, the curve was crippled, the taper was interrupted; the lichen ate the vigour of the stock, and the ivy slowly strangled to death the promising sapling.

Yet, as Grace, during Fitzpiers's absence, falls in love with Giles again,

> he rose upon her memory as the fruit-god and the wood-god in alternation: sometimes leafy and smeared with green lichen, as she had seen him amongst the sappy boughs of the plantations: sometimes cider-stained and starred with apple-pips. . .

And in a later poem, "The Pine Planters", subtitled "Marty South's Reverie", Hardy describes Marty and Giles:

> We work here together
> In blast and breeze ;
> He fills the earth in,
> I hold the trees…

There is almost a continuum between the prose of *The Woodlanders* and many of Hardy's poems. At times he feels for trees as much as for people: they almost *are* people, simultaneously creative and destructive, beyond rational explanation.

But *The Woodlanders*, being a novel, is a vehicle for concerns which Hardy, as a radical minded man of the late 19th century wished, characteristically, to express. Its rational core (its poetic core is elsewhere, in half intuited rituals from Celtic and Anglo-Saxon woodland paganism) is an exploration of how difficult it is for Grace to obtain a divorce, according to the latest laws, from Fitzpiers once he has abandoned her, and thus to marry Giles. It turns out to be impossible. And although there is room for the usual quibbles in such matters as to whether Hardy was or was not "anti-marriage" – the same quibbles which arise from *Jude the Obscure*, and *Two on a Tower* – there is no room for doubt that his view on divorce was a century ahead of its time: that it should be freely available on the grounds of what would now be called "breakdown of the marriage."

It is hard to be sure where Hardy's own life lurks in this densely tangled novel. As usual, he occupies emotionally both sides of a pair of rivals. That there is something of him in the stoical, Anglo-Saxon, sexually reticent Winterbourne is without doubt. But there is also much of him in the fickle, womanising, seductive, and philosophical Fitzpiers. A telltale sign is that, like the villain Manston in *Desperate Remedies*, he articulates Hardyan reflections: "he told me that no man's hands could help what they did, any more than the hands of a clock." And critics who assume that Grace's rekindling of her marriage at the end of the novel is a disaster (as her hidebound father Melbury thinks: "It's a forlorn hope for her; and God knows how it will end!") may be being more moralistic than Hardy himself: a careful reading of the ending shows firstly that Grace is still sexually aroused by Fitzpiers, and secondly that he has become aware of deeper feelings for her than he has experienced for women before. Admittedly, they move away from the woodlands to the Midlands but possibly this will free them up for a "new" life. In the last analysis, Fitzpiers has been brought to his own feelings by the power of the feelings in Grace.

Perhaps *The Woodlanders* was Hardy's favourite because in it he came closest to a balance between his own two halves. Winterbourne is an animist, absorbed into nature. Fitzpiers is a rationalist, distinct from nature. Winterbourne accepts nature, can change nothing, is only aware of the continuum between life and death and so cannot wilfully choose life, or even struggle against death. Fitzpiers tinkers with nature, manipulates it as he experiments with women, distinguishes, as a doctor, between life and death, and as a man wilfully possesses life and rejects death. All this, for both men, through women of course who pay, through their suffering, as Hardy's women paid.

There is something in Grace of Elizabeth-Jane in *The Mayor of Casterbridge*, as there is something of Henchard in the rough and ambitious Melbury. Grace is pushed around by her father and therefore, at first, by Fitzpiers but she comes through to her strength, expressed most clearly in a single sentence: "I am what I feel, father."

As always, the names of characters are revealing. Fitzpiers is a Norman name, meaning "Piers' son" cf. Pierston, also Hardy-like, and suggesting the strength of a rock ("pierre") as well as phallic piercing, in *The Well-Beloved*. His first name, though is the Anglo-Saxon "Edred", meaning "noble-speaking" ie he is a smooth talker. His rival's names are neatly opposite in origin, the first name Giles being Norman, and Winterbourne being Anglo-Saxon – appropriate to a figure who is almost mythical (those discussions with Barnes again?), who is both "born in winter", like a sacred king (cf. Jesus), and a "winter-bourne", a stream which is only visible in winter, by definition chilly. They are brought together, in a sense, through their very different loves for the aptly named "Grace", who after being "disgraced", redeems the errant son of the spear. (He "fits" his spear very nicely, as Felice ["Happy"] and Suke Damson [ripe as a plum] could testify).

If such conjectures seem far-fetched, the novel itself can be consulted. It says more about the relation of sex and emotion than most novels, but delicately enough (or cunningly enough) not to cause scandal in the same way that *Tess* and *Jude* did. (It was even a set book on first level English courses in the late 1950s…) The delicacy is in the language. For example, when it is reported that Fitzpiers has been thrown from his horse and injured, all three women whom he has slept with (Suke, Felice, and Grace) find themselves together. Grace contemplates the other two:

> "He is dying, perhaps!" blubbered Suke Damson, putting her apron to her eyes.
> In their gestures and faces there were anxieties, affection, agony of heart – all for a man who had wronged them – had never really behaved towards either of them anyhow but selfishly. Neither one but would have well-nigh sacrificed half her life to him, even now. The tears which his possible critical situation could not bring to her eyes surged over at the contemplation of these fellow-women whose relations with him were as close as her own without its con–ventionality. She went out to the balustrade, bent herself upon it, and wept.

Some critics have seen Grace as colourless, but she is no more so than Elizabeth-Jane. Both are quiet, but capable of wisdom. Yes, Hardy himself was, as Seymour-Smith rightly concludes his biography in the words of Marty South at Winterbourne's grave, "a good man, and did good things." But his poems and novels show a remorseful awareness that he could also be a bad man, especially with women. It is the thankless task, he senses, of a woman such as Grace to bring these two halves together.

Hardy's "rustic chorus", typically, provide a more accepting conclusion than Marty's vigil by the grave. Two pages previously, a conversation about Grace and Fitzpiers occurs in the village pub, The Three Tuns:

> "But this deceiving of folks is nothing unusual in matrimony," said Farmer Cawtree. "I know'd a man and wife – faith, I don't mind owning, as there's no strangers here, that the pair were my own relations – they'd be at it that hot one hour that you'd hear the poker, and the tongs, and the bellows, and the warming-pan, flee across the house with the movements of their vengeance; and the next hour

> you'd hear 'em singing "The Spotted Cow" together, as peaceable as two holy twins; yes – and very good voices they had, and would strike in like street ballet-singers to one another's support in the high notes.

## *Tess of the Durbervilles*

In *Tess of the Durbervilles,* Alex Durberville is a Fitzpiers gone rotten – a seducer beyond redemption, though he turns to preaching redemption. He is like a wife-beater who buys the wife flowers, a sado-masochist, not only a psychopath but a moaner: he blames Tess for the evil he does to her. When she stabs him and his blood drips through the ceiling there is no drop of sympathy for him in the reader as there would be for Fitzpiers or for Sergeant Troy, or even for the organ-playing Manston.

Angel Clare is Winterbourne gone icy inert, unable to respond. Although as his name suggests (a clear angel), he has something in common with Gabriel (the archangel) Oak. But Oak is always able to forgive Bathsheba for going with Troy. Angel cannot forgive Tess until it is too late, and even then his forgiveness is lukewarm: at best he is a Laodicean, and Hardy did not like Laodiceans. At the end of the novel, Angel's intimacy with Tess's look-alike but bland sister, Liza Lou, is actually disgusting to many readers, much worse than the marriage, faked or not by Hardy, between Thomasin and Venn at the end of *The Return of the Native.*

Since the two male members, as it were, of the triangle in Tess are such total failures, this draws attention inevitably and almost exclusively to Tess herself. The fact that most readers call *Tess of the Durbervilles* simply *Tess*, as Hardy himself usually did, shows how much the novel has succeeded in becoming her story – that of "A Pure Woman" as its outrageous subtitle stated. A pure woman who has been defiled, bears a bastard child who dies, deceives her future husband, eventually murders her former lover, then sleeps with her rediscovered husband during the days she is on the run from the law, and then finally is hanged: pure? But her purity, as Hardy's delicate writing about her, or through her, makes clear, is in her naive faith in herself and, unfortunately, in her husband. No matter what she experiences, she remains innocent like the lamb in Blake's poems. And her innocence, Hardy makes clear, includes sexual desire and satisfaction, Tess's "invincible instinct towards self-delight".

Tess is Hardy's great suffering heroine – as archetypal as Brecht's Mother Courage, and more compelling. Yet the novel, *her* novel, was still called *Tess of the Durbervilles.* The *of* reinforces the fact of her ownership and control by two men: her wastrel father, Jack Durbeyfield, and her vicious seducer, Alex Durberville. The fact that Alex's family name is a bought one, and he is not a Durberville at all, reinforces the message: his main trait, even, is that he is not noble in character as Tess is, but ignoble. At the rational, non-poetic level, Hardy as usual succeeds in conveying a sharp anger at what the world does to women, at Victorian moralism, and the total failure of Christianity to apply its own precepts or even to believe in itself. (Victorian England contained many Anglican priests who seem to have carried through Shelley's project of becoming ordained without believing in God). Although as usual Hardy expresses biting anger at parsons (it is a parson, with the usual obsession with hierarchy, and heedlessly self-indulgent with words, who starts the whole tragedy moving by greeting the wretchedly drunken Jack Durbeyfield as "Sir John"), he is too profound to see this failure as anything but tragic. He refers – following a theme he took up again in *Jude the Obscure* – to "the chronic melancholy which is taking hold of the civilised races with the decline of belief in a beneficent power."

Delighting in Tess so much that when he was in his early 80s he had to fall in love with the young Dorset actress who played her in a stage version, Hardy fondly explores her psychology, with a delicacy and lack of prurience which are rare when men write about women. Here is Tess after breast-feeding the child she has had by Alex:

> When the infant had taken its fill the young mother sat it upright in her lap, and looking into the far distance dandled it with a gloomy indifference that was almost dislike; then all of a sudden she fell to violently kissing it some dozens of times as if she could never leave off, the child crying at the vehemence of an onset which strangely combined passionateness with contempt.

And here is Hardy, who supposedly never fathered a child, showing a subtle awareness of the continuum between sex and mothering: Tess shows her love for her child exactly as Alex has shown his "love" for her. And she has been caught by Alex. As an observing country-woman remarks,

> She's fond of that there child, though she mid pretend to hate 'en.

An equally observing reader might conclude that Tess is "ambivalent" about Alex. But part of her purity is that she is never ambivalent: what she does, she feels. And she always knows herself. (One sub-theme in this novel is that an uneducated woman may be much more intelligent than an educated man.) As she says to Alex:

> "I have never really and truly loved you, and I think I never can." She added mournfully, "Perhaps, of all things, a lie on this thing would do the most good to me now; but I have honour enough left, little as 'tis, not to tell that lie. If I did love you, I may have the best o' causes for letting you know it. But I don't."

Her love for Angel, by contrast, is total. And here, in this passionately pure woman, is her tragic flaw: she accepts male values. She is not robust enough to do otherwise. Here is where the education which could make a free woman like Paula Powers could have given Tess the confidence of her intelligence. But as always, the intelligence is at work:

> Her idolatry of this man was such that she herself almost feared it to be ill-omened… "O my love, my love, why do I love you so!" she whispered there alone; "for she you love is not my real self, but one in my image; the one I might have been!"

And soon after this realisation, as Tess and Angel set off in a carriage on their wedding trip, in the middle of a sunny afternoon, the farm cock settles on the fence and begins to crow. "It only means a change in the weather," remarks the farmer's wife to her husband; "not what you think: 'tis impossible!" The impossible thought is cuckoldry. The omens for tragedy are in place. And the timing of such events is so apt in Hardy, rendering them credible, because they seem part of a seamless web of events. For Hardy the animist, space and time were a continuum some while before Einstein demonstrated this (and Hardy liked Einstein). The concluding remark of the novel that "Justice was done, and the President of the Immortals, in Aeschylean phrase, had ended his sport with Tess", reveals Hardy the intellectual ironist. And its concluding event, the hanging of Tess in the gaol, is marked only indirectly, by the raising of a black flag on the gaol tower. The emotional and poetic conclusion occurs a few pages earlier, when Tess and Angel, exhausted by their flight from her pursuers, end up in Stonehenge, and she spreads herself out to sleep on one of the slabs.

> He knelt down beside her outstretched form, and put his lips upon hers.
> "Sleepy are you, dear? I think you are lying on an altar."
> "I like very much to be here," she murmured. "It is so solemn and lonely after my great happiness with nothing but the sky above my face."

After they have talked for a while, Tess asks,

> ... "Tell me now, Angel, do you think we shall meet again after we are dead? I want to know." He kissed her to avoid a reply at such a time.
> "O Angel – I fear that means no! said she, with a suppressed sob. "And I wanted to see you again – so much, so much! What – not even you and I, Angel, who love each other so well?"
> Like a greater than himself, to the critical question at the critical time he did not answer; and they were again silent. In a minute or two her breathing became more regular, her clasp of his hand relaxed, and she fell asleep. The band of silver paleness along the east horizon made even the distant parts of the Great Plain appear dark and near... The eastward pillars and their architraves stood up blackly against the light, and the great flame-shaped Sun-stone beyond them; and the Stone of Sacrifice midway. Presently the night wind died out, and the quivering little pools in the cup-like hollows of the stones lay still. At the same time something seemed to move on the verge of the dip eastward, a mere dot. It was the head of a man approaching them from the hollow beyond the Sun-stone...

This is unbearable. (Though the decent English policemen, at Angel's urging, wait "still as the pillars around" until Tess wakes up, before arresting her.) Hardy might well finish the novel, for civilisation's sake, with a quip about the Greek "Immortals", but his feelings are with an older paganism than the Greek and much older than the Christianity which cynically arouses expectations about "meeting in heaven" which a rational man like Angel can hardly accept, even under pressure. But in her last revealed moment before Tess disappears into custody,

> "It is as it should be," she murmured. "Angel, I am almost glad – yes, glad! This happiness could not have lasted. It was too much. I have had enough; and now I shall not live for you to despise me!"

> She stood up, shook herself, and went forward, neither of the men having moved.
> "I am ready," she said quietly.

In spite of the self-sacrifice, and the apparent acceptance of guilt and of Angel's scheme of values, this is not quite a Christian sentiment. She has suffered enough, and knows it: "I have had enough" of suffering, surely, as well as the brief happiness about which she is supposed to feel guilty. And by now she knows her man: yes, Angel will despise her, because of what she has done. But she does not despise herself. She is ready. Her nobility, at this moment, in the pagan setting from which she derives, returns her to it. Her tragedy has been that she has had to believe in others' (men's) values, and (like Ethelberta and Bathsheba) she has been unable to find a language to express her own values. So we do not know what they are anymore than we know what values lie behind Stonehenge. Tess simply *is.* And although her character is in no way like what we know of Emma Hardy's, there is a clue in what Hardy most valued in Emma, to what he most values in Tess: she is so *living.*

### *Jude the Obscure*

Hardy wrote one of his disingenuous Prefaces to the first edition of *Jude the Obscure* stating the novel was "simply an endeavour to give shape and coherence to a series of seemings, or personal impressions..." But in a Postscript sixteen years later he was able to report that "its next misfortune was to be burnt by a bishop probably in his despair at not being able to burn me." He then goes on to a discussion of divorce: "My opinion at that time, if I remember rightly, was what it is now, that a marriage should be dissolvable as soon as it becomes a cruelty to either of the parties being then essentially and morally no marriage." But this is a red herring. In truth, *Jude the Obscure* is more about marriage than divorce (which is hardly discussed in it) or perhaps more exactly about "no marriage", in that the one relationship in the book which approximates to the Christian ideal of marriage is the living together of Jude and his cousin Sue in a love which is often chaste (she enjoys sex, but not always, and deprives him of it for long periods, out of fastidiousness), and which produces children. Jude's actual marriage to the sluttish Arabella begins under false pretences (she tells him falsely that she is pregnant), and lasts only a few months, although they do fall into bed together many years later, and resume a sordid relationship of despair on Jude's side, opportunism on hers. But this has been set up from the start, by marriage itself. As Hardy describes the ceremony, "the two swore that at every other time of their lives till death took them, they would assuredly believe, feel, and desire precisely as they had believed, felt and desired during the few preceding weeks."

Their one child, known as Father Time, has been born in Australia, and Jude does not even meet him or know he exists until he is aged ten, and rejected by Arabella. Jude and Sue, although living in hardship, take him in, and eventually he hangs himself and their children "Because we are too menny." He is, as has been pointed out by many critics, "thoroughly modern" (meaning late $20^{th}$/ early $21^{st}$ century, a social work case, and clinically depressed). Similarly, Sue is "thoroughly modern", a feminist struggling with her ambivalence about sex and men. It is not usually noted that Arabella, who receives a bad press from critics who do not seem to relish, as Hardy does, her animal vitality, is also "thoroughly modern", a fun-loving girl who neglects her son, lives off other people's benevolence, and has an alcohol problem.

In the midst of all this is the issue of Jude, an intelligent country boy who studies Latin and Greek when long days of toil permit him to (he has been inspired by a schoolmaster, Phillotson, who turns out to be a creep and a hypocrite: Sue marries him, just to make a moral point, then leaves him for Jude), but who cannot gain admission to Christminster (in effect, Oxford). Nowadays this is a non-issue, as it was even when *Jude the Obscure* was written. (Ruskin College, Oxford, had already been founded, and offered scholarships to working men, which was a start.) But the dissonance between Jude's background and his aspirations and interests is real enough, as it was to Hardy. Jude wants to go to Christminster, but he is intelligent enough (more intelligent, it is made clear, than most of its academic denizens) to see, for example, that "mediaevalism was as dead as a fern-leaf in a lump of coal." It is not every stonemason who reflects when he is attracted to a girl, as Jude is to Sue:

> "After all," he said, "it is not altogether an *erotolepsy* that is the matter with me, as at that first time. I can see that she is exceptionally bright; and it is partly a wish for intellectual sympathy, and a craving for loving-kindness in my solitude."

Hardy is teasing his hero here. Nevertheless, in the real world in which Hardy and Emma lived, the novel caused them both suffering. Emma was no fool, and saw that it was not about divorce (about which, though an Anglican, she seems to have had liberal views) but about marriage. It contributed to the ruin of theirs. Or, more exactly, the ruin inherent in Hardy's views, once made explicit in a novel, could no longer be denied.

These were the problems of Hardy the rationalist, alive in his own age. But the problems of Hardy the animist were no less acute. *Jude the Obscure* turns *Tess of the Durbervilles* upside down. The two male rivals who have appeared in many of his novels and approach their essences as Alex and Angel are now eliminated. The nauseating Phillotson is no match for Jude. This is Jude's novel, as the previous novel was Tess's. And instead of two male rivals combining to destroy a naive and intelligent woman, here are two female rivals combining to destroy a naive and intelligent man. Jude simply fades away and dies at the end, as unconvincingly from the medical point of view as Giles Winterbourne, although alcoholic despair is a factor, since, abandoned by Sue in her despair at the deaths of their children, and reunited cynically with Arabella who flirts with and is preparing to sleep with other men, he cannot survive.

The two women are as much opposites as Alex and Angel and, of course, in their inner selves as much similar: both are controlling, only the means differ.

Arabella controls through sex. She is described in animal terms ("She was a complete and substantial female animal – no more, no less") and more exactly as a pig: she is expert at butchering pigs (hence the pizzle she throws at Jude) and is compared at one point to a "flitch" or side of ham. But she is irresistible. Perhaps it is Celtic: her name is Arabella Donn suggesting Welshness, as well as Donne's carnal love poems, and "dun" complexioned as used by Shakespeare for the sensual Dark Lady in his Sonnets. And, in the kind of hidden word-play for which Hardy seldom receives credit, she is a Donn, as opposed to a university Don such as Jude wants to become. After Jude has met her, "an indescribable lightness of heel served to lift him along." As for Arabella, honest in her own way, she confides to a friend, "I shall go mad if I can't give myself to him altogether!"

Sue Brideshead (suggesting the pure Susanna of the Bible who rejects the lecherous advances of the Elders, as well as maidenhead and virginity) is seen by Jude has having an "epicene" (sexless) tenderness. "What a comrade she would make… She was nearer to him than any woman he had ever met." She has previously lived, daringly but chastely, with a student who has died partly, it seems, out of frustration at not being able to have her. "You mustn't love me. You are to like me that's all," she tells Jude. For a long while he does not dare tell her his story, about Arabella. When at last he does, she says

> "Why didn't you tell me before!"
> "I couldn't. It seemed so cruel to tell it."
> "To yourself, Jude. So it was better to be cruel to me!"

So she cuts through him like a knife. "Sue, you are terribly cutting when you like to be a perfect Voltaire!" She is intellectually active, and thinks for herself. He is intellectually passive, absorptive of book-learning. She does risk all for him, and they make love and have children, but she rejects "relations based on animal desire", and prefers "the wide field of strong attachment where desire plays, at least, only a secondary part."

The dialogues between Jude and Sue are intellectually compelling, and surely new in literature when they were written. The encounters between Jude and Arabella are sexually compelling, and similarly new. But they are completely incompatible ways of being in the world. No wonder Jude is torn apart as if Arabella and Sue are the Furies.

Jude's tragedy is overtly that he is "obscure": he never fulfils his ambitions. But his obscurity goes further than this: his understanding remains obscure, in spite of his intellect, since he cannot reconcile the forces represented by Arabella and Sue. In a sense, Arabella is also obscure: she cannot explain herself intellectually, and her sexual irresistibility, which can prevail even when Jude finds her repulsive, is, as always in such cases, obscure. And Sue, with her clear intellect, admits to a tragic obscurity. "I talked to the child as one should only talk to people of a mature age. I said the world was against us, that it was better to be out of life than in it at this price; and he took it literally." Yet she has been evasive about the facts of life – about sex, which makes her uncomfortable, just as thought makes Arabella uncomfortable – in not explaining to Father Time why she and Jude, in spite of their poverty, go on having more children. "I wasn't truthful, for with a false delicacy I told him too obscurely."

Sue anguishes to Jude about her fatal dialogue with Father Time, "Why didn't I tell him pleasant untruths, instead of half-realities?" There is an assumption here, that sexual love (which after all has produced Father Time as much as any other human being) is not "pleasant". If Hardy ever wanted to affirm sexual love, he might have done so here, but he does not. His poems wonderfully record the "seemings" of life, but there is a lack somewhere in his experience. Perhaps his novels reflect a personal tragedy (not an uncommon one) that sexual passion and emotional affinity have not occurred for him with one and the same person. *Jude the Obscure* contains several joking passages involving Sue and Father Time about the *appearance* of marriage being purely negative: if a couple are seen fighting, they are married, and if harmonious they are not.

The intellectually liberated Sue and the stunted Father Time share the same bleak view of life: their brains, their Central Nervous Systems, are compatible. But their emotional make-ups, their Autonomic Nervous Systems, are not. Sue bounces or springs along like fluff, "flexible and light as a bird... went along as if she hardly touched ground." Father Time moves in a "steady mechanical creep which had in it an impersonal quality – the movement of the wave, or of the breeze, or of the cloud." Father Time, as his name suggests, is a kind of First Cause (not unlike the God who appears in Hardy's gnostic think-piece poems), an automaton (rationalism as Necessity) who knows that flowers will wither and sees Oxford Colleges (accurately enough) as gaols. He is, like the God in Hardy's poems, a "somnambulist" – not entirely conscious, and emotionally dead. Hardy, who vowed as a young man to live life "as emotion", ended with a novel in which an automaton (made so by lack of love from his fun-loving mother) hangs his foster brothers and sisters *for a reason*: "We are too menny." And since Father Time, long before his existence on suburban weathervanes, has been traditionally accepted as being God, Hardy in this novel is saying bluntly that God kills children.

Again, as in *Tess of the Durbervilles,* in *Jude the Obscure* we are faced with unbearable pain. It seems Hardy has gone as far as he can go. In turn he has explored to the limit the two extremes of a man (himself) through Alex and Angel as they combine to destroy a woman, and now the two sides of woman through Arabella and Sue as they combine to destroy a man (himself). What more is there for him to say in a novel? *The Well-Beloved,* though finished and published the year after *Jude the Obscure,* is merely an intellectual tidying up of a self-satirical novel begun earlier. In *Tess* and *Jude,* to call them by their simplest names, Hardy has come through to the two opposing truths about men's effect on women, and women's effect on men, which he has been working towards in his previous novels. The animist in Hardy understood human suffering as intrinsic to nature, but still cried out against it. The rationalist in him tried to explain it through think-piece poems about a God who did not care, or through attacks on society's institutions – education, marriage, the church. In his last two novels (*The Well-Beloved* does not count), he has pursued suffering to its limit, from both perspectives in himself.

The reception of *Jude the Obscure* was indeed abominable, triggered by an attack in New York (by a woman, one Jeanette Gilder) which said Hardy was "disgusting" and his mind "seems to run on pigs animal and human", and followed in London by a review headed *Jude the Obscene.* But although Hardy liked to foster the myth that he had stopped writing novels because of this reception of *Jude,* or that he was now ready to turn back to poetry, the truth is surely that he had said what he had to say as a novelist, and he had never stopped being a poet.

# 7 Middle Poems (1875-1909)

Hardy liked to assume his poems were ephemeral, no more likely to last than those "seemings" of which life was made. At the age of 81 he wrote that they were "a series of impressions which I have never tried to coordinate." And he never said much on the subject of language in itself – perhaps a sensitive subject for him in view of yet another duality in his life: the correct English he spoke in public and with his wives co-existed with the Dorset dialect he spoke in private with his family of origin and William Barnes, and seldom acknowledged, although he did tip his hat to it when he compared it to the German he heard spoken by prisoners of war he made a point of visiting in Dorchester. He saw English, at any rate, as perpetually changing, and when he had a plaque installed in Stinsford church to commemorate the church musicians among whom his father and grandfather had played, he made sure it was in Latin: it had more chance of lasting. So when he sees fit to give poems titles in Latin, this is a sign that he takes them seriously. Such are the great sequence "In Tenebris" (1895-6), and the cluster of poems after Emma's death (1912-13) which he headed with the quote from Horace, "Veteris vestigia flammae" (Vestige of an old flame). Along with "Wessex Heights" (1896) and "In Front of the Landscape" which are frankly in the first person as well as being long, declamatory and grand, these poems are the most easily given the vulgar, but sometimes indispensable, term "great." Many of them are also given importance by being put either at the beginning or end of volumes or sections: Hardy knew which of his poems were the most powerful, although he seems to have been ready to give any of them a chance.

His best poems may at first be hard to discern in the huge accumulation of both good and bad, inspired and artificial, poems in which they are embedded – the hills and valleys of the Hardyan landscape. And he did not make the task easier when he added to his habits of elusiveness in dating old poems, and placing poems out of context as decoys, various formal claims to the effect that, as he put it in the brief Preface to *Wessex Poems,* "The pieces are in a large degree dramatic or personative in conception ; and this is even where they are not obviously so." This drab statement contains at least two booby traps: first the word "personative", which Hardy has invented for the occasion and which seems to mean "only pretending to be written by the person who utters them", with the sub-hint of "impersonation"; and secondly the "even when they are not obviously so" – ie, "even if you think the 'I' of these poems is me, it probably isn't." And for *Time's Laughingstocks* (1909) he wrote that his poems in the first person should be regarded as "dramatic monologues by various characters."

These subterfuges should not be despised, being necessary for most poets who write anything other than safe public verse, but they should be disregarded in a reading of the poems. Where poems feel to the reader impassioned, it is likely that they are autobiographical, as indeed some of them can be demonstrated to be – which is not important in itself so much as proof of the integrity of these very powerful poems which lurk among the various verse compositions of the Hardyan landscape, and which the reader who goes through the poems more than once will come to recognise.

This book can make no attempt to catalogue the best of Hardy's poems: there are too many of them. But some attempt will be made to provide the reader with a few guidelines in his or her work in sorting them out.

Hardy's Middle poems can be conveniently defined as those written up to and including *Time's Laughingstocks* (1909), but excluding those Early poems, mainly the Weymouth poems, which are either dated, or by internal evidence can be clearly dated, between 1865 and 1872. His next volume, *Satires of Circumstance*, 1914, contains the sequence of poems after the death of Emma, and starts the final cycle, as it were, of his poetic life: most poems from this and subsequent volumes can be considered as Late poems but, as usual with Hardy's complicated bibliography, the volumes which appeared in 1914 and later also include, again either dated or datable, poems from between 1872 and 1909, ie Middle poems. Poems sub-labelled "Weymouth", though often undated, appear here and there up to his latest volumes. The very best new Hardy edition would be one that was accurately in chronological order.

Hardy's poems include a variety of genres: short lyrics in the first person (usually "personative" only in the sense that the speaker may be Hardy himself or a woman with whom he is in relation); lyrical poems which may be longer and which contain dramatic dialogues (again usually from Hardy's personal life); narrative poems which are like short stories in verse; narrative poems which either are described as Ballads or have a ballad metre, and which are very much "art ballads" (deriving via Coleridge and the romantics from the late 18th century German "Kunstballaden" which many readers will know from their settings by Schubert or Schumann); philosophical think-pieces which discuss mainly Hardy's view of God as a sort of

Demiurge who has lost both power over and interest in the world he has created (these might as well have been written in prose); various set pieces on famous people or places; unashamedly public poems on Wars or other stirring events, such as the sinking of the Titanic; some that he described as "flippant, not to say farcical pieces"; and of course epitaphs whether of people or of animals.

Before discussing several quite powerful poems, here is an example of a very bad one. (It would be a worthy candidate for Quiller-Couch's *Oxford Book of English Verse*). "Genoa and the Mediterranean", March 1887, begins:

> O epic famed, god-haunted Central Sea,
> Heave careless of the deep wrong done to thee
> When from Torino's track I saw thy face first flash on me.
>
> And multi-marbled Genoa the Proud,
> Gleam all unconscious how, wide-lipped, up-browed,
> I first beheld thee clad – not as the Beauty but the Dowd...

This is the kind of thing that any Victorian tourist might be moved to *want* to write – not actually moved to write. This is almost as bad as when in "The Lost Pyx" Hardy describes cows gathering around as "Blackmore's hairy throng." (Of course the bad poems of a good poet, if we are lucky enough to see them before they are junked, can be instructive about the differences between poetry and verse). But even Hardy's set pieces can sometimes come up golden when they touch something deeply personal in him, for example his brave but painful free-thinking about religion, as in "Lausanne. In Gibbon's Old Garden", written June 27, 1897, "the 110th anniversary of the completion of the "Decline and Fall" at the same hour and place". This dense 16 line poem, which ends with a wonderfully slanted re-phrasing of a quote from Milton (*"Truth like a bastard comes into the world / Never without ill-fame to him who gives her birth")*, reveals something of Hardy the intellectual, as well as the exquisite, and by our standards modern, oblique rhyme of the 1st and 4th lines of the opening stanza:

> A spirit seems to pass,
> Formal in pose, but grave withal and grand :
> He contemplates a volume in his hand,
> And far lamps fleck him through the acacias.

Hardy would have paid special attention to the acacias: in Peacock's biography of Shelley there is a quotation from a letter by Shelley describing how in 1816 he and Byron visited Gibbon's garden and Byron to the disapproval of Shelley (who did not believe in picking plants any more than Hardy believed in "wounding" trees) gathered some acacia leaves as a souvenir.

Some of Hardy's think-pieces about his view of God are quite savage, as for example a late poem "An Inquiry" in which a rather thick and absent minded God is referred to throughout as "It". (No wonder bishops fulminated against him...) A rather typical statement of his usual theme is "God's Education":

> I saw him steal the light away
> That haunted in her eye:
> It went so gently none could say
> More than that it was there one day
> And missing by-and-by.
>
> I watched him longer, and he stole
> Her lily tincts and rose;
> All her young spriteliness of soul
> Next fell beneath his cold control,
> And disappeared like those.
>
> I asked : "Why do you serve her so?
> Do you, for some glad day,
> Hoard these her sweets – ?" He said, "O no,
> They charm not me ; I bid Time throw
> Them carelessly away."
>
> Said I: "We call that cruelty –
> We, your poor mortal kind."
> He mused. "The thought is new to me.
> Forsooth, though I men's master be,
> Theirs is the teaching mind!"

This is an argument worthy of Shelley, whose idealism-turned-against-God influenced Hardy greatly, but it is handled with much more finesse: the anger which was often so shrill and hysterical in Shelley is controlled and focused by irony in Hardy. (Also by his knowledge of the Gnostic tradition: Seymour-Smith's biography is particularly illuminating of this.) But, at bottom, philosophy works against poetry (it ruined Shelley's) because its medium is generalisation rather than what Blake called "the minute particular". Although Hardy's poem is touching in the particulars of the woman's decay, it becomes wooden and stylised as emotion deserts it and is replaced by the poem's *point* towards which Hardy has been too consciously working.

Hardy's poems on public events inevitably tend to endure no longer than the immediate memory of the events themselves. He seems to have written them out of a sense of having to do his duty – especially as too old to be a combatant in the Boer War or the First World War, both of which tormented him. The famous "In Time of The Breaking of Nations", published during the First World War in 1915, but based on lines written in 1870, during the Franco-Prussian War, is moving precisely because in a time of public events, it concentrates on the "minute particular" (originally of a scene on a walk with Emma in St Juliot):

> Only a man harrowing clods
>     In a slow silent walk
> With an old horse that stumbles and nods
>     Half asleep as they stalk . . .

Similarly, "Drummer Hodge" sums up the Boer War through a particular death:

> I
>
> They throw in Drummer Hodge, to rest
>     Uncoffined just as found:
> His landmark is a kopje-crest
>     That breaks the veldt around;
> And foreign constellations west
>     Each night above his mound.

———— ————

> III
>
> Yet portion of that unknown plain
>     Will Hodge forever be;
> His homely Northern breast and brain
>     Grow to some Southern tree,
> And strange-eyed constellations reign
>     His stars eternally.

This animism with a vengeance remains superior, though much less well known, to the high-flown rhetoric of Rupert Brook's famous "There is some corner of a foreign field / That is forever England", which is derived from it.

Given Hardy's predilections for a good death (he famously, in extreme old age, had to be restrained from recounting to a young girl the details of the burning of a supposed witch hundreds of years before, which he had been reading about – in particular the bursting of her breasts, which were full of milk since she had been nursing a child), his epitaph poems might be expected to be grim indeed. However, as in his poem about his grandmother, "One We Knew", written in 1902, he is more often ready to take the long view, to see the life in terms of a time. And here we see, instead of as so often the poet in the novelist, the novelist in the poet:

> ...With cap-framed face and long gaze into the embers –
> We seated around her knees –
> She would dwell on such dead themes, not as one who remembers,
> But rather as one who sees.
>
> She seemed one left behind of a band gone distant
> So far that no tongue could hail:
> Past things retold were to her as things existent,
> Things present but as a tale.

Hardy grew up among country songs and ballads: Dorset and Somerset, the core of his Wessex, were the main hunting grounds of the great Victorian folksong collectors, Sharp, Baring-Gould, and Hammond. He would certainly have known "O No John", with the cheerful lecherousness of

> Madam shall I tie your garter
> Tie it a little above your knee?
> If my hand should slip a little farther
> Would you think it amiss of me?
> O No John, No John, No John No...

and "The Foggy Dew", which in some versions ends with the young girl's lover living alone with their son. Both seem to combine in Hardy's gruesome "The Dark-Eyed Gentleman", of which these are the 1st and 3rd stanzas:

I pitched my day's leazings in Crimmercrock Lane,
To tie up my garter and jog on again,
When a dear dark-eyed gentleman passed there and said,
In a way that made all o' me colour rose-red,
        "What do I see
        O pretty knee!"
And he came and he tied up my garter for me...

... Yet now I've beside me a fine lissom lad,
And my slip's nigh forgot, and my days are not sad;
My own dearest joy is he, comrade and friend,
He it is who safe-guards me, on him I depend;
        No sorrow brings he,
        And thankful I be,
That his daddy once tied up my garter for me.

It is hard to believe that the novelist who wrote so frankly of sex in *Jude the Obscure* and *The Woodlanders*, and who humorously introduced bawdy double-meanings into supposedly innocent scenes in *Two on a Tower*, could write in this squirmingly coy way; and still harder to believe that Hardy the ultra-realist could be guilty of such sentimentality. But "sentimentality is a failure of feeling," and Hardy's true feeling fails him in most of his art-ballads because he is laying on the art rather than the ballad: he is, uncharacteristically, trying to please his readers.

Yet again and again he was drawn to writing art-ballads if not in the Wessex folk style, in the Border Ballad style, as in the grotesquely titled "The Vampirine Fair":

Gilbert had sailed to India's shore,
        And I was all alone :
My lord came in at my open door
        And said, "O fairest one!"

He leant upon the slant bureau,
        And sighed, "I am sick for thee!"
"My Lord," said I, "pray speak not so,
        Since wedded wife I be...

Perhaps all this is simply an infection of Victorian horror, but it is puzzling. Did Hardy perhaps associate true folksong and ballads with the nights of dancing and debauchery he attended with his father as a child with his violin, and find himself unable to either resist or acknowledge their attraction? He had shown what he could do with a traditional narrative poem in the riotous "The Bride-Night Fire", but he largely abandoned this tone along with any idea of writing, like his beloved Barnes, in Dorset dialect. Besides which "The Bride-Night Fire", written nostalgically from London by a naive countryman of 26, displayed not so much an immoral quality but, more dangerous, an amoral one, which he may have preferred to leave behind although he did have the courage to publish it (somewhat bowdlerized as noted) in *Wessex Poems*. In comparison, Hardy's art-ballads are a sort of taking on of the Victorian singing robes which is best forgotten.

More striking to most readers than any of the rather self-conscious, it seems, *genre* poems with which Hardy kept his hand in, are the immediately personal ones – those he claimed were "personative", and may have been pleased to smuggle into collections of more artificial pieces which he thought would attract his readers more. There are too many of these personal poems to list: they are the heart of his work. An example in the 1902 volume is "A Broken Appointment", which sums up his frustrated effort to make love to Florence Henniker, and even permits itself what seems to be the traditional pun on the word "come" which is not usual in Hardy (whose poems tend to be lucidly clear rather than multi-levelled) but never to be ruled out (remember the outrageous double-meanings in *Two on a Tower*), and another pun on "dear" as both beloved and costing (pain), and on hour / our (the "hope-hour" being for the longed for time and the longed for "our". There may be other double-meanings in the first stanza of this poem, suggested by the images of being worn numb, of "stroked its sum": its *some* perhaps, as well as its sum.

> You did not come,
> And marching Time drew on, and wore me numb –
> Yet less for loss of your dear presence there
> Than that I thus found lacking in your make
> That high compassion which can overbear
> Reluctance for pure lovingkindness' sake
> Grieved I, when, as the hope-hour stroked its sum,
> You did not come.

Like others of Hardy's most personal poems, this is, if not blatantly multi-leveled (like, say, a poem by Donne or Blake), extremely condensed. It sees the love episode from at least two angles: as, yes, a betrayal of sexual expectation which leaves Hardy literally alone with his own flesh; but also as a betrayal of something which for Hardy was of wider importance: "loving kindness" the core of the only moral scheme he would permit himself.

The poem which follows "A Broken Appointment" in the volume is "Between Us Now", which exemplifies another key quality in Hardy's personal (*not* personative) poems: a fairly intricate rhyme scheme and metre which nevertheless are handled in a totally natural and conversational style. And if even the Victorian reader might have found some words, such as "wont" for "are accustomed too" a little old-fashioned, this is not an adopted "poetic diction": Hardy actually was, to many who met him, a little old-fashioned in talk and manner. He was, after all, a countryman, though capable of much smoothness:

> Between us now and here –
>     Two thrown together
> Who are not wont to wear
>     Life's flushest feather –
> Who see the scenes slide past,
> The daytimes dimming fast,
> Let there be truth at last,
>     Even if despair...

Finally, Hardy's middle poems include two of those usually considered to be "great poems". The first is "Wessex Heights", written in 1896 when he had made his decision to write no more novels and to turn only to poetry, but held back and slipped into the midst of *Satires of Circumstance* (1914).

This poem of resolution seems to have cost him dear: in it he resolves to maintain his vision, from the heights of poetry, as it were, to remain above real places, people, and ghosts. The poem is both proud and sad. Hardy's most grand utterings are usually in long lines of 7 or 8 stresses: these demand a sustained pitch of intensity to come off, as they do in these great poems. It is as if when Hardy takes the long view he is taken over by long lines.

"In Tenebris" (In the darkness, Psalm xx, Authorized Version) has three parts, each preceded by a quote, in Latin, from the psalms. Part I is in short line quatrains:

Wintertime nighs;
But my bereavement-pain
It cannot bring again:
Twice no one dies.

Flower-petals flee;
But, since it once hath been,
No more that severing scene
Can harrow me...

A poet does not choose a metre: rather, the metre chooses the poet. (Or if this seems too mystical: from the store of metres the poet has absorbed in his or her lifetime, one will emerge and impose itself on the theme which emotionally it best fits.) Hardy may have known, clearly or dimly, that this bracketing of two six syllable lines by two four syllable lines, was reminiscent of medieval Latin verse which (he will not have known) in its turn is reminiscent of the Old Irish verse which was spread into Latin speaking Europe, after the decline of the Roman Empire, by Irish monks. Classical (Latin and Greek) verse was quantitative, each line consisting of a number of "feet", usually five or six, each containing two or three "long" and "short" syllables, arranged in accepted patterns. Irish (and probably other Celtic) verse was syllabic, each line consisting of a given number of syllables, and the poem often consisting of quatrains with lines of 4, 5, 6 or 7 syllables in a regular pattern. English verse, although it has been subjected to manipulation along Classical lines is stress-based: although Classicists may call Shakespeare's blank verse an "iambic pentameter", it is in fact a variable five stress line.

The metre of Hardy's "In Tenebris", part I, however, is entirely syllabic, each syllable is almost equally stressed (as reading the poem aloud in a natural voice will demonstrate), and there is no variation whatsoever in the syllable count. The effect is hypnotic, emotionally intense, original in English: the almost equally stressed syllables in regular short lines convey finality: the end. It is almost the same metre as one of the earliest Old Irish poems, the address by the woman poet Liadan (in effect the Old Irish Sappho) to her poet lover Cuirithir whom she is renouncing: the end.

After this quite extraordinary emergence of a metre from Celtic and Celticized Latin verse, parts II and III of "In Tenebris" emerge in long (up to 20 syllables) 7 stress lines, in rhymed pairs, which have their origins in medieval English verse, and are reminiscent of ballad metres where alternating four and three stress lines would amount to 7 stress lines if not for the rhymes which end each four or three stress line. Hardy's view is suddenly the long one. From the intense personal suffering of the "one" in part I, he now moves to how this suffering is created by the rejection of others. In Part II, as in "Wessex Heights", he turns his difference from others into defiance (as after all he must, to survive) as this Part ends with a kind of Credo, even as he is forced out on his own. And in the man who defiantly "disturbs the order here" we can recognise the Hardy not only of the poems but the novels:

> Let him in whose ears the low voiced Best is killed by the clash of the First,
> Who holds that if way to the Better there be, it exacts a full look at the Worst,
> Who feels that delight is a delicate growth cramped by crookedness, custom and fear,
> Get him up and be gone as one shaped awry ; he disturbs the order here.

In Part III he goes back to scenes from his childhood, when he might, as a sickly child, have died, but for "she who upheld me" a dim reference to his mother: "Confident I in her watching and ward through the blackening heather / Deeming her matchless in might and with measureless scope endued..." He concludes the poem, "Then might the Voice that is law have said "Cease !" and the ending have come." And each stanza of Part III describes how the ending could have come during any moment of life when he worked on the flowerbeds in Spring, when "in the midmost of Egdon" he felt upheld by his mother, or when he was "the smallest and feeblest of folk there". If the poem is "about" something, it is how to survive when death can strike at any moment as we know it can, if we bother to think about it. (Hardy bothered...) And of course it cannot provide a solution: there is none. Yet the bleak finality of Part I is succeeded by a more expansive sense of defiance in Part II, and then a series of visions, as it were, in Part III, which are so fully alive that although this is surely one of the most gloomy poems ever written, it is also in an unexpected way, one of the most hopeful.

Martin Seymour-Smith, biographer of both Hardy and Robert Graves, has remarked that some lines of Graves's (in "A Country House", 1937)

> A smell of mould from loft to cellar,
> Yet sap still brisk in the oak
> Of the great beams: if ever they use a saw
> It will stain, as cutting a branch from a green tree

are "some of the loveliest lines of hope written in this century." The same can be said of Hardy's reaffirmation of order, if only a seeming one, in Part III of "In Tenebris":

> ... on the noon when the half-sunny hours told that April was nigh,
> And I upgathered and cast forth the snow from the crocus border,
> Fashioned and furbished the soil into a summer-seeming order,
> Growing in gladsome faith that I quickened the year thereby.

# 8 Short Stories and *The Dynasts*

Hardy published three collections of short stories, *Wessex Tales* (1888), *A Group of Noble Dames* (1891), and *Life's Little Ironies* (1894). Some are well known: "The Melancholy Hussar", reminiscent of the scene of *The Trumpet Major;* "The Withered Hand" about the woman who is brought by the hangman to cure her mysteriously withered arm (she feels she has been cursed) by placing it on the corpse of a hanged man who turns out to be her son; "Fellow Townsmen", about a love that is at first illicit then so timid that it is never realised. Although vivid, they are not as enthralling as the novels. He wrote then at so many guineas a word, for magazines, and they are the prose equivalent of his verse think-pieces, pursuing an idea sometimes almost clinically to its conclusion.

For example, "On the Western Circuit" is about a lawyer from London whose work brings him to Melchester (Salisbury) where he is attracted to a pretty servant girl whom he observes on a merry-go-round and subsequently seduces, with a technical skill which may recall Hardy's own efforts as a young man: "Not content with holding the hand, he playfully slipped two of his fingers inside her glove, against her palm" a very old signal of sexual desire. His seduction succeeds, and she becomes pregnant. There would be no question of him marrying her, but she has begun a correspondence with him in which the letters are written, as a favour to her, by her employer, a plain but intelligent and frustrated married woman who has seen the lawyer from a distance and become infatuated with him. The letters cause the lawyer to believe he is truly in love with the servant girl, and they are married – immediately after which he discovers that she can only write a few lines "in the characters and spelling of a child of eight, and with the ideas of a goose." He must accept the marriage (as must the girl's now ex-employer who has almost forgotten her own husband in the heat of this love affair by letter with a stranger), and the story ends with

> "What are you doing, dear Charles?" she said timidly from the other window, and drew nearer to him as if he were a god.
> "Reading over all those sweet letters to me signed "Anna,", he replied with dreary resignation.

Now, there may be a message here about the general horrors of marriage, or about a particular dilemma Hardy felt about being attracted to a "she-animal" (as Anna is described) who does not have a mind. But the story must be read for itself. And it is a frigid and cynical piece of work. Often, unfortunately, Hardy's short stories do not live up to the intensity of his novels, because they are too dominated by their initial idea: he does not seem to stay with them long enough to be carried away by them. They are passing flings with ideas, as it were, not relationships.

Where they are not frigid, Hardy's short stories are often dragged down by a despair which seems total because the form requires it to be so brusque: there is no room for the animistic intimations of *life* which give some hope in his novels. His short stories seem to be written entirely from his rationalistic side, though in the few that are memorable ("The Withered Arm" is probably the best known) the animistic side comes through.

An anomaly among Hardy's works is a long story (or short novel) for children, *Our Exploits at West Poley*, which he wrote in 1883 for a Boston magazine *Youth's Companion*, but which was lost in obscurity until revived in a new edition in 1952. In it he returns to the *sententiae* which marred his early novels, as if he cannot resist trying to get his world view across to his prospective readership of young boys:

> "The straight course is generally the best for boys... Be sure that professions you know little of have as many drudgeries attached to them as those you know well."

Here Pooter speaks. But the story is much more interesting than its *sententiae.* It is about two boys (a villager and his visiting cousin) who clamber into a cave in the Mendip Hills where nobody has ever gone before and discover a spring in a cavern, which they block, for fun, with rock. As a result, the water supply of the village dries up but the arid village down the road is suddenly blessed with a new spring, and the economies of the two villages reverse themselves. The boys – though this is not stated overtly have in effect become gods who can decide which village will benefit from water supply. The inhabitants of both villages almost go to war in a paroxysm of territorial greed and rivalry. In the end events turn out well (no pun intended): the story tells how. But this

> is by the merest chance in the world. Your courage is praiseworthy, but you see the risks that are incurred when people go out of their way to meddle with what they don't understand... Quiet

> perseverance in clearly defined courses is, as a rule, better than the erratic exploits that may do much harm.

The speaker is known as "The Man Who Failed". He has emigrated from his village decades before, in the hope of a better life, but returned, defeated but not unhappy. One of the boys, Steve, says, "He has failed in life, and how can his opinions be worth anything?" His mother replies:

> For this reason… He is one who has failed, not from want of sense, but from want of energy; and people of that sort, when kindely [sic] are better worth attending to than those successful ones, who have never seen the seamy side of things.

These *sententiae*, in contrast with the witty examples in the early novels, which seem designed to show Hardy at his most urbane and sophisticated, seem written more from his animistic side. Their morality is more pagan than Christian: if the Good Samaritan had decided not to "meddle", the man in the ditch would have been left to die. Hardy's perspective, his guard apparently let down, in *Our Exploits at West Poley*, is undoubtedly conservative, but in a pagan way: it is wrong to meddle with the flow of natural things; if you try to help someone you will be sucked in to their ill-fortune; and if you put your energy into material success you have no chance of ever being wise. Above all, don't play God – says the future author of *Tess of the Durbervilles*.

### *The Dynasts*

In his huge (three parts, 19 acts, 131 scenes, verse in 30 different rhyme schemes, prose drama and narrative, stage directions) unclassifiable work *The Dynasts*, published between 1903 and 1908, Hardy took up the theme he had enounced in *The Trumpet Major* in 1880: Napoleon "the mighty little man who was less than human in feeling, and more than human in will."

*The Dynasts* has its champions, and it has remained in print although not in paperback, and mint editions of the hardback can be found in second hand bookshops. It is difficult to "place". Is it just another failed Edwardian epic poem, like Robert Bridges' *The Testament of Beauty?* Or a completely mad work like the suspiciously similar-sounding, and thankfully lost, verse epic on the subject of Waterloo written by Emma Hardy's brother, confined to a lunatic asylum? Or a precursor of the 20th century radio play? It was broadcast five times on the BBC, between 1933 and 1967, and is perhaps most effective as what the Germans call a *Hörspiele* a "hear-play." A critic, Susan Dean, has demonstrated its affinities with what the Victorians called a "diorama" and which exists in some museums: stuffed animals or historical personages are displayed against a sweeping highlit background. The essence is a bird's eye view appropriate to this period of Hardy's life when his marriage was disintegrating, his attempts to find a new woman were unsuccessful, and he was physically ill, resembling "an ancient moulting eagle."

A problem is that *The Dynasts* disappoints expectations at every level. Its prose passages, about the ordinary people of Dorset preparing for Napoleon's invasion, are vivid but not as vivid as when his "rustic chorus" appears in his novels. Its blank verse passages about the debates in the House of Commons or about the battle of Waterloo are clearly written but often drab and not as rhythmically alive as Shakespeare in, say, *Henry IV, Parts I & II.* The blank verse exchanges, typeset in Italics, among the "Spirit Ironic", the "Spirit Sinister", the "Spirit of the Pities" and "The Spirit of the Years" et al. are philosophically original, yet not so succinct as similar passages in Hardy's more didactic poems, and marred by archaisms: "Why doth he go?" etc. The stage directions are extensive and detailed, but often banal and Pooteresque ("He provisionally throws a regal air into his countenance"). The more extended directions or *mises-en-scène* which describe the main shifts in the action are often compelling in their vision but awkwardly phrased:

> It turns to a day of drowsing heat. and the Emperor draws a deep breath as he shifts his weight from one puffed calf to the other. The light cavalry, the foot, the artillery having passed, the heavy horse now crosses, their glitter outshining the ripples on the stream.
> A messenger enters. NAPOLEON reads papers that are brought, and frowns.

The scope of the vision from the puffed calves of Napoleon's legs to the glitter of the cavalry on the stream is wonderful. But "now crosses, their glitter" may seem grammatically clumsy not only to pedants, and "papers that are brought" is frustrating: who or what brings them?

*The Dynasts* runs to over 700 pages. What is memorable? – only a few disparate elements: the scenes of the Dorset country people lighting their beacons in a false alarm; the surprisingly interesting blank verse exchanges among the politicians Pitt and Fox and their King; the rapid switching back and forth of the scene from one side to another at Waterloo, and the character of Wellington, hating war but fighting it brilliantly.

But these are all characteristically *English* scenes. The success of *The Dynasts* is in its patriotism. Its stated theme – Napoleon who wants to rule the world but is in fact ruled by forces beyond his control – fades more quickly from the mind. It is no accident that two out of the five BBC broadcasts of *The Dynasts* were done during the Second World War.

The play (or drama, or "work": it is impossible to say what exactly it is) also contains one extraordinary and famous passage of poetry. (This out of hundreds of pages of blank verse: it is all very well to quote Coleridge, as Seymour-Smith does, to the effect that a long work in verse cannot be all poetry, but in *The Dynasts* the proportion of poetry to verse is minuscule. Hardy's prose, in his later novels, contains more poetry than the verse in *The Dynasts).* Here is the field of Waterloo, seen and felt by Hardy the animist, leaving his preplanned drama aside:

*Yea, the coneys are scared by the thud of hoofs,*
*And their white scuts flash at their vanishing heels,*
*And swallows abandon the hamlet roofs.*

*The mole's tunnelled chambers are crushed by wheels,*
*The lark's eggs scattered, their owners fled ;*
*And the hedgehog's household the sapper unseals.*

*The snail draws in at the terrible tread,*
*But in vain ; he is crushed by the felloe-rim ;*
*The worm asks what can be overhead,*

*And wriggles deep from a scene so grim,*
*And guesses him safe ; for he does not know*
*What a foul red rain will be soaking him !*

*Beaten about by the heel and toe*
*Are butterflies, sick of the day's long rheum,*
*To die of worse than the weather-foe.*

*Trodden and bruised to a miry tomb*
*Are ears that have greened but will never be gold,*
*And flowers in the bud that will never bloom.*

In truth, Hardy had never been to war, had never been present at political conferences, had never met a king or a queen, had never been to Austria or Russia, and his boasted connection with the Captain Hardy who kissed Nelson and who figures largely in *The Dynasts* was spurious. But he had grown up among Dorset people who were descendants of those who lit the beacons between Weymouth and Dorchester, he loved England in every fibre of his body, and he was an instinctive animist who felt for the sufferings of animals and even insects, or trees for that matter, as much as for the sufferings of people. What works in *The Dynasts* is not what is derived from his reading, from his wish to be like Shakespeare, from the Edwardian compulsion to do something big in verse, or even from his long fascination with the Napoleonic Wars, which is far more movingly expressed in *The Trumpet Major.* What works is his love of England, his capacity to take the long view and to ask large questions, and the poem quoted above. Not until Isaac Rosenberg wrote "Dead Man's Dump" in 1917 (a year before he was killed, his own corpse never recovered) was there another poem quite like it.

If Hardy had gone to war, like Tolstoy, perhaps he could have written the English equivalent of *War and Peace*. Or even, if he had confined himself to straightforward historical description he might have written a prose narrative that was moving – as for example accounts of the English (meaning also Scottish and Irish) sailors methodically setting the rigging on the *Victory* as it and they were repeatedly blown away by cannon balls can bring tears to the eyes. Instead, *The Dynasts* may impress, but it is seldom moving. Hardy is too much outside himself. But there remains that poem…

# 9 Late Poems (1909-1928)

So far as Hardy ever permitted himself to put his cards on the table, he did so at the age of 81, in the foreword which, however, he labelled an "Apology" to *Late Lyrics and Earlier*, 1922.

> In any event poetry, pure literature in general, religion – I include religion, in its essential and undogmatic sense, because poetry and religion touch each other, or rather modulate into each other ; are, indeed, often but different names for the same thing – these, I say, the visible signs of mental and emotional life, must like all other things keep moving, becoming...

And

> It may indeed be a forlorn hope, a mere dream, that of an alliance between religion, which must be retained unless the world is to perish, and complete rationality, which must come, unless also the world is to perish, by means of the interfusing effect of poetry – "the breath and finer spirit of all knowledge ; the impassioned expression of science," as it was defined by an English poet who was quite orthodox in his ideas.

In other words poetry, far from being the mere "fugitive impressions" he had always liked to claim, might actually through its ability to interfuse religion and science be the world's last hope! Hardy is going back to his poetic roots in Shelley, who saw poets as "the unacknowledged legislators of mankind", and was for most of his life (there were signs he might be changing toward more realism, from the general to the particular, in the poems written for Jane Williams just before he was so uselessly drowned at the age of 29) more enthused by wilfully (and destructively, as it turned out) inspiring others, than by allowing poetry to inspire him. Hardy's "forlorn hope", at the least an acknowledgement that for him poetry had "interfused" the two sides of his nature, is more modest than Shelley's, more realistic, more hard won.

Hardy's late poems encompass most of the genres explored in earlier years, with no sign of diminishing powers. After all, his collections had always been uneven, as he acknowledged in his 1922 "Apology" through the tongue in cheek discussion of "the chance little shocks that may be caused over a book of various character… by the juxtaposition of unrelated, even discordant effusions ; poems perhaps years apart in the making yet facing each other . . .. [so that the reader is ] unconscious that he is laughing with the author and not at him." Tongue in cheek because Hardy knew very well that he could have chosen to arrange his poems chronologically, or by theme, or by person addressed, or in any other order – if he had wanted to reveal more of himself.

In *Satires of Circumstance* (1914) and later volumes, Hardy allows occasional glimpses of scenes which recall much earlier poems but which are perhaps less autobiographically revealing out of context. "I Rose Up as My Custom Is" is in the words of a ghost revisiting a former love

> … As she lay by her husband's side ;
> I asked her if life pleased her, now
> She was rid of a poet wrung in brow,
> And crazed with the ills he eyed…

She tells him,

> "You were a poet – quite the ideal
> That we all love awhile:
> But look at this man snoring here –
> He's no romantic chantecleer,
> Yet keeps me in good style.
>
> "He makes no quest into my htoughts,
> But a poet wants to know
> What one has felt from the earliest days,
> Why one thought not in other ways,
> And one's Loves of long ago."
>
> Her words benumbed my fond, faint ghost…

Not wonderful poetry, but like many of Hardy's less successful poems this at least provides some insight into his life: this sounds like the Weymouth relationship, clearly summarised.

But it was when Emma died that he allowed himself to burst free of his usual camouflage and to reveal much of his relationship with her, by first clustering together 21 poems written soon after her death and labelling them *Veteris vestigia flammae*, and then including other shorter clusters which are clearly, from the similar imagery, also in memory of her.

The picture painted by some writers on Hardy, of him pent up alone in his study writing poems to Emma while his second wife Florence quarrelled hysterically with the servants downstairs, is an exaggeration which ignores one of the disturbing facts about poetry – that it chooses its own subjects and insists on telling its own story, no matter what its supposed author wishes. Florence was important in Hardy's life: neurotic, yes, but supportive, cheering (her complaining has also been exaggerated), and his sexual partner until almost the end of his life. He inscribed her copy of *Moments of Vision* (1917), "to the first of women, Florence Hardy."

Some of his pleasure in her is conveyed in a cluster of poems, "After the Visit", "To Meet, or Otherwise", and "The Difference", from around 1910 when she was secretly his mistress: her "presence is as a leaf that skims / Down a drouthy way", her feet are "light on the green as a thistledown ball", she has "large, luminous living eyes", she is the "girl of my dreams", his "Heartmate."

Perhaps Hardy would have preferred to sit in his study writing love poems which he could bring downstairs as little presents for Florence – not writing anguished, desperately longing and regretful, romantically loving poems to the stubborn, eccentric and difficult Emma, whom he had at times wished dead, and who had died without warning before he was able to make his peace with her. Florence, without a doubt, would have preferred this too. But this is not the way poetry works.

Poetry is also, in a sense "outside time" – the opposite of a novel in this sense. For Hardy, taken over by the poems to Emma, a moment from forty years before was as vivid as one from only a year or so before, and no doubt (if he was like other poets) poems sparked by incidents decades apart could press to be written within a few days or even hours of each other. The relative jumble of the *Veteris vestigia flammae* is wholly natural then, for once not a camouflage: these are all poems about Hardy and Emma, as much about what might have happened as about what did – in both instances causing a regret which is particular and personal but which accumulates so that the poems of this cluster, and the various later ones that belong with it, narrative in their particulars but not in the whole as a novel would be, form a single, long episodic poem.

Whether, as in "Overlooking the River Stour", he is regretting not paying attention to Emma "Never I turned my head, alack, / While these things met my gaze... / To see the more behind my back ..." or in "The Last

Performance" not understanding why, a few days before her unexpected death, he found Emma at the piano – "I am playing my oldest tunes," declared she, / "All the old tunes I know..." – the domestic details accumulate into what is, in effect, a multi-poemed elegy to a particular woman whose character, difficult as it was, enters into the poems as much as Hardy's own:

It was your way, my dear,
To vanish without a word
When callers, friends or kin
Had left, and I hastened in
To rejoin you, as I inferred.

And when you'd a mind to career
Off anywhere – say to town
You were all of a sudden gone
Before I had thought thereon,
Or noticed your trunks were down.

So, now that you disappear
For ever in that swift style,
Your meaning seems to me
Just as it used to be:
"Goodbye is not worthwhile!"

This intimate little poem in the *Veteris vestigia flammae* cluster is fairly typical of most of his poems to Emma. But occasionally there is a more impassioned howl which lifts a poem out of the cumulative elegiac collection into the same world of intensity as the great long-lined poems, and Emma, though still herself ("even to the original air-blue gown") becomes more than herself, and Hardy, for that matter, more than himself. "The Voice" is one of those key poems in the "Muse" tradition of the poet's absolute need for the woman he loves as the source of his inspiration. The voice, which at the end in the poet's despair at his woman's loss has become only a "wind oozing thin through the thorn", as the incantatory metre suddenly runs out and the lines become short of breath, is poetry itself.

Woman much missed, how you call to me, call to me,
Saying that now you are not as you were

When you had changed from the one who was all to me,
But as at first, when our day was fair.

Can it be you that I hear? Let me view you, then,
Standing as when I drew near to the town
Where you would wait for me : yes, as I knew you then,
Even to the original air-blue gown !

Or is it only the breeze, in its listlessness
Travelling across the wet mead to me here,
You being ever dissolved to wan wistfulness,
Heard no more again far or near ?

Thus I ; faltering forward,
Leaves around me falling,
Wind oozing thin through the thorn from norward,
And the woman calling.

Hardy decided to end his last volume of poems, *Winter Words*, which in fact appeared posthumously, with "He Resolves to Say No More", written in 1927. He is making the kind of grim point he liked to make, but the implied readers are too much in evidence and the poem is mannered:

O my soul, keep the rest unknown!
It is too like a sound of moan
When the charnel-eyed
Pale Horse has nighed :
Yea, none shall gather what I hide…

A more fitting epitaph for himself is the miraculous "Afterwards", probably written sometime between 1913 and 1916, which ends *Moments of Vision* (1917). Another long liner of sustained intensity, its beginning in particular conveys the essence of the man – the huge self confidence of an "ecstatic temperament" coexisting with an extreme delicacy of feeling and perception which must have been his since his earliest years at that conjunction of fields, woods and heath where he was born:

When the Present has latched its postern behind my tremulous stay,
And the May month flaps its glad green leaves like wings,
Delicate-filmed as new-spun silk, will the neighbours say,
"He was a man who used to notice such things" ?

Hardy's great long-line poems are about himself. His love poems often have the urgency of shorter lines throughout, or, like "The Voice" are in 5 stress lines which shorten to an urgent ending. Although the long-line poems are easily described as "great" because of their incantatory mode, and the relentless taking stock of life and himself in them, his *Complete Poems* reveal to the reader that Hardy is, somewhat unexpectedly, one of the great love poets in English. The delicate attention to "minute particulars" that is essential to Hardy's nature as "Afterwards" shows, is also apparent in his love poems. Why are they not immediately identifiable as love poems? Perhaps because they are first of all poetry, not a subtype of it, but perhaps also because Hardy eschews generalisation, to the extent that his vocabulary contains almost no abstractions. (He was the opposite of his beloved Shelley in this). This great love poet almost never uses the word "love."

# Selected Bibliography

## Works by Hardy

*Collected Poems of Thomas Hardy* Macmillan, London, 1930. This is the first edition to collect all the poems, and has been reprinted frequently between 1930 and now. *Complete Poems* and *Variorum Edition*, edited J Gibson, in the New Wessex Edition, Macmillan, London, 1976 and 1979, and in 3 volumes *The Complete Poetical Works of Thomas Hardy* edited S Hynes, Oxford University Press, 1982-85 are also available, as is a super-cheap but serviceable paperback edition by Wordsworth Classics. But the original Macmillan edition, with its red binding and green cover, though the poems are cramped together on the pages and in smallish type, remains a favourite to many, and continues the format adopted during Hardy's lifetime.

The Wessex Edition of Hardy's works, which was begun by Macmillan in 1912, includes all the novels, and *The Dynasts*. The New Wessex Edition, of the 1970s, also Macmillan, is newly edited and annotated, and still in print in both hardback and paperback. *The Short Stories of Thomas Hardy* were first collected by Macmillan in 1928, and have similarly been reprinted.

Currently, as well as the Macmillan paperbacks, there is a paperback edition of Hardy's works by Oxford University Press (World Classics series), and a cheap edition by Wordsworth Classics.

Readers will follow their own taste in choosing from the above. The Wordsworth editions have minimal introductions and the same text as the Macmillan editions (Hardy is out of copyright). The OUP and Macmillan Editions are both attractive, but the quality of the introductions and notes varies widely (and the Macmillan hardback editions' use of bold asterisks to indicate references may be irritating to many). Particularly good ones are Alan Manford's OUP edition of *A Pair of Blue Eyes,* and Geoffrey Grigson's New Wessex edition of *Under the Greenwood Tree.*

## Hardy's Life

The main biographies are by Robert Gittings, *Young Thomas Hardy* and *The Older Hardy,* London 1975 and 1978; Michael Millgate, *Thomas Hardy*: *A Critical Biography,* London 1982; and Martin Seymour-Smith, *Hardy,* London 1994.

Millgate's biography efficiently disposes of Gittings's more speculative theories, and is solid as a rock but, as it were, slimy with the seaweed of undeclared emotion. Perhaps a clue to the pressing need of the main academic biographers, Gittings and Millgate, to show their superiority to Hardy is pique at his attitude to critics such as themselves. Gittings permits himself a *cri de coeur* about Hardy's "ruling obsession about the critics" and concludes: "Hardy was to... produce a mean-minded attack on critics while actually lying on his death-bed." Well, perhaps Hardy knew...

Seymour-Smith is more prolix, certainly more idiosyncratic, but having paid his own dues to poetry he is able to go to the heart of what made Hardy a poet – which is to say what made him himself. Like Seymour-Smith's biography of Robert Graves, his *Hardy* is written from critical love, not pseudo-critical envy. It is also unusually astute psychologically, perhaps because of its open approach in which a sense of indignation, affection, or disappointment as the case may be, is allowed to show itself along with analytic rigour.

## Other Works

No attempt can be made here to summarise or evaluate the hundreds of critical studies of Hardy, which range from the academic text (increasingly ideological in the 1990s) to the coffee table picture book. For basic reference, Purdy's *Thomas Hardy, A Bibliographical Study*, London 1954, and F. B. Pinion's *A Thomas Hardy Dictionary,* London 1989, are useful.

# GREENWICH EXCHANGE BOOKS

## STUDENT GUIDES

Greenwich Exchange Student Guides are critical studies of major or contemporary serious writers in English and selected European languages. The series is for the Student, the Teacher and the 'common reader' and are ideal resources for libraries. The *Times Educational Supplement (TES)* praised these books saying, "The style of these guides has a pressure of meaning behind it. Students should learn from that... If art is about selection, perception and taste, then this is it."

(ISBN prefix 1-871551- applies)
*The series includes:*
**W. H. Auden** by Stephen Wade (-36-6)
**William Blake** by Peter Davies (-27-7)
**The Brontës** by Peter Davies (-24-2)
**Joseph Conrad** by Martin Seymour-Smith (-18-8)
**William Cowper** by Michael Thorn (-25-0)
**Charles Dickens** by Robert Giddings (-26-9)
**John Donne** by Sean Haldane (-23-4)
**Thomas Hardy** by Sean Haldane (-35-1)
**Seamus Heaney** by Warren Hope (-37-4)
**Philip Larkin** by Warren Hope (-35-8)
**Shakespeare's Non-Dramatic Poetry** (22-6)
**Tobias Smollett** by Robert Giddings (-21-8)
**Alfred Lord Tennyson** by Michael Thorn (-20-X)
**Wordsworth** by Andrew Keanie (57-9)

## OTHER GREENWICH EXCHANGE BOOKS

All paperbacks unless otherwise stated.

## POETRY

**Adam's Thoughts in Winter** *by Warren Hope*
Warren Hope's poems have appeared from time to time in a number of literary periodicals, pamphlets, and anthologies on both sides of the Atlantic. They appeal to lovers of poetry everywhere. His poems are brief, clear, frequently lyrical, characterised by wit, but often distinguished by tenderness. The poems gathered in this first book-length collection counter the brutalising ethos of contemporary life, speaking of and for the virtues of modesty, honesty, and gentleness in an individual, memorable way. Hope was born in Philadelphia where he raised his family and continues to live near there. He is the author of

critical studies of Shakespeare and Larkin and is the biographer of Norman Cameron, the British poet and translator.
ISBN 1-871551-40-4; A5 size; 54pp

**Baudelaire: Les Fleurs du Mal in English Verse**
*translated by F. W. Leakey*
Selected poems from *Les Fleurs du Mal* are translated with parallel French texts, are designed to be read with pleasure by readers who have no French, as well as those practised in the French language.
F. W. Leakey is Emeritus Professor of French in the University of London. As a scholar, critic and teacher he has specialised in the work of Baudelaire for 50 years. He has published a number of books on Baudelaire.
ISBN 1-871551-10-2; A5 size; 140pp

**Lines from the Stone Age** *by Sean Haldane*
Reviewing Sean Haldane's 1992 volume *Desire in Belfast* Robert Nye wrote in *The Times* that 'Haldane can be sure of his place among the English poets.' The facts that his early volumes appeared in Canada and that he has earned his living by other means than literature have meant that this place is not yet a conspicuous one, although his poems have always had their circle of readers. The 60 previously unpublished poems of *Lines from the Stone Age* – 'lines of longing, terror, pride, lust and pain' – may widen this circle.
ISBN 1-871551-39-0; A5 size; 58pp

**Wilderness** *by Martin Seymour-Smith*
This is Seymour-Smith's first publication of his poetry for more than 20 years. This collection of 36 poems is a fearless account of an inner life of love, frustration, guilt, laughter and the celebration of others. Best known to the general public as the author of the controversial and best selling *Hardy* (1994).
ISBN 1-871551-08-0; A5 size; 64pp

## LITERATURE & BIOGRAPHY

**The Author, the Book & the Reader** *by Robert Giddings*
This collection of essays analyses the effects of changing technology and the attendant commercial pressures on literary styles and subject matter. Authors covered include Dickens; Smollett; Mark Twain; Dr Johnson; John Le Carré.
ISBN 1-871551-01-0; A5 size; 220pp; illus.

**English Language Skills** *by Vera Hughes*
If you want to be sure, as a student, or in your business or personal life, that your written English is correct and up-to-date, this book is for you. Vera Hughes' aim is to help you remember the basic rules of spelling, grammar and punctuation.

‘Noun’, ‘verb’, ‘subject’, ‘object’ and ‘adjective’ are the only technical terms used. The book teaches the clear, accurate English required by the business and office world, coaching in acceptable current usage, and making the rules easier to remember.
With a degree in modern languages and trained as a legal secretary, Vera Hughes went from the City into training with the retail industry before joining MSC as a Senior Training Advisor. As an experienced freelance trainer, she has worked at all levels throughout the UK and overseas, training business people in communication skills, but specialising in written business English. As former Regional Manager for RSA Examinations Board, she is also aware of the needs of students in schools and colleges. Her sound knowledge of English and her wide business experience are an ideal combination for a book about basic English language skills.
ISBN 1-871551-60-9; A5 size; 156pp.

**The Good That We Do** *by John Lucas*
John Lucas’s new book blends fiction, biography and social history in order to tell the story of the grandfather he never knew. Horace Kelly was born in Torquay in 1880 and died sixty years later, soon after the outbreak of the second world war. Headteacher of a succession of elementary schools in impoverished areas of London during the first part of the 20th century, “Hod” Kelly was also a keen cricketer, a devotee of the music hall, and included among his friends the great Trade Union leader, Ernest Bevin. In telling the story of his life, Lucas has provided a fascinating range of insights into the lives of ordinary Londoners: their entertainments, domestic arrangements, experiences of the privations of war, including the aerial bombardments of 1917 and 1918, and their growing realisation during the 1920s and 1930s that they were doomed to suffer it all again. Threaded through is an account of such people’s hunger for education, and of the different ways government, church and educational officialdom ministered to that hunger. *The Good That We Do* is both a study of one man and of a period when England was changed, drastically and for ever.
ISBN 1-871551-54-4; A5 size, 218pp

**In Pursuit of Lewis Carroll** *by Raphael Shaberman*
Sherlock Holmes and the author uncover new evidence in their investigations into the mysterious life and writing of Lewis Carroll. They examine published works by Carroll that have been overlooked by previous commentators. A newly discovered poem, almost certainly by Carroll, is published here. Amongst many aspects of Carroll’s highly complex personality, this book explores his relationship with his parents, numerous child friends, and the formidable Mrs Liddell, mother of the immortal Alice.
ISBN 1-871551-13-7; 70% A4 size; 130pp; illus.

**Laughter in the Dark – The Plays of Joe Orton** *by Arthur Burke*
Arthur Burke examines the two facets of Joe Orton. Orton the playwright had a rare ability to delight and shock audiences with such outrageous farces as *Loot* and *What the Butler Saw*. Orton the man was a promiscuous homosexual caught up in a destructive relationship with a jealous and violent older man. In this study – often as irreverent as the plays themselves – Burke dissects Orton's comedy and traces the connection between the lifestyle and the work. Previously a television critic and comedian, Arthur Burke is a writer and journalist. He has published articles not only on Orton but also on Harold Pinter, John Osborne and many other leading modern dramatists.
ISBN 1-981551-56-0; A5 size 100pp

**Liar! Liar!': Jack Kerouac – Novelist** *by R. J. Ellis*
The fullest study of Jack Kerouac's fiction to date. It is the first book to devote an individual chapter to each and every one of his novels. *On the Road, Visions of Cody* and *The Subterraneans*, Kerouac's central masterpieces, are re-read indepth, in a new and exciting way. The books Kerouac himself saw as major elements of his spontaneous 'bop' odyssey, *Visions of Gerard* and *Doctor Sax*, are also strikingly reinterpreted, as are other, daringly innovative writings, like 'The Railroad Earth' and his 'try at a spontaneous *Finnegans Wake'*, *Old Angel Midnight*. Undeservedly neglected writings, such as *Tristessa* and *Big Sur*, are also analysed, alongside better known novels like *Dharma Bums* and *Desolation Angels*.
*Liar! Liar!* takes its title for the words of *Tristessa's* narrator, Jack, referring to himself. He also warns us 'I guess, I'm a liar, watch out!'. R. J. Ellis' study provocatively proposes that we need to take this warning seriously and, rather than reading Kerouac's novels simply as fictional versions of his life, focus just as much on the way the novels stand as variations on a series of ambiguously-represented themes: explorations of class, sexual identity, the French-Canadian Catholic confessional, and addiction in its hydra-headed modern forms. Ellis shows how Kerouac's deep anxieties in each of these arenas makes him an incisive commentator on his uncertain times and a bitingly honest self-critic, constantly attacking his narrators' 'vanities'.
R. J. Ellis is Professor of English and American Studies at the Nottingham Trent University. His commentaries on Beat writing have been frequently published, and his most recent book, a full modern edition of Harriet Wilson's *Our Nig*, the first ever novel by an African American woman, has been widely acclaimed.
ISBN 1-871551-53-6; A5 size; 300pp

**Norman Cameron** *by Warren Hope*
Cameron's poetry was admired by Auden; celebrated by Dylan Thomas; valued by Robert Graves. He was described by Martin Seymour-Smith as one of… the most rewarding and pure poets of his generation…" and is at last given a full length

biography. This eminently sociable man, who had periods of darkness and despair, wrote little poetry by comparison with others of his time, but always of a high and consistent quality – imaginative and profound.
ISBN 1-871551-05-6; A5 size; 250pp; illus.

**Musical Offering** *by Yolanthe Leigh*
In a series of vivid sketches, anecdotes and reflections, Yolanthe Leigh tells the story of her growing up in the Poland of the nineteen thirties and the second world war. These are poignant episodes of a child's first encounters with both the enchantments and the cruelties of the world; and from a later time, stark memories of the brutality of the Nazi invasion, and the hardships of student life in Warsaw under the Occupation. But most of all this is a record of inward development; passages of remarkable intensity and simplicity describe the girl's response to religion, to music, and to her discovery of philosophy.
The outcome is something unique, a book that eludes classification. In its own distinctive fashion, it creates a memorable picture of a highly perceptive and sensitive individual, set against a background of national tragedy.
ISBN 1-871551-46-3; A5 size 61pp

**Shakespeare's Non-Dramatic Poetry** *by Martin Seymour-Smith*
In this study, completed shortly before his death in 1998, Martin Seymour-Smith sheds fresh light on two very different groups of Shakespeare's non-dramatic poems: the early and conventional *Venus and Adonis* and *The Rape of Lucrece*, and the highly personal *Sonnets*. He explains the genesis of the first two in the genre of Ovidian narrative poetry in which a young Elizabethan man of letters was expected to excel, and which was highly popular. In the *Sonnets* (his 1963 old-spelling edition of which is being reissued by Greenwich Exchange) he traces the mental journey of a man going through an acute psychological crisis as he faces up to the truth about his own unconventional sexuality.
It is a study which confronts those 'disagreeables' in the *Sonnets* which most critics have ignored.
ISBN 1-871551-22-6; A5 size; 90pp

**Shakespeare's Sonnets** *edited by Martin Seymour-Smith*
Martin Seymour-Smith's outstanding achievement lies in the field of literary biography and criticism. In 1963 he produced his comprehensive edition, in the old spelling of *Shakespeare's Sonnets* (here revised and corrected by him and Peter Davies in 1998). With its landmark introduction, it was praised by William Empson and John Dover Wilson. Stephen Spender said of him: "I greatly admire Martin Seymour-Smith for the independence of his views and the great interest of his mind;" and both Robert Graves and Anthony Burgess described him as the leading critic of his time. His exegesis of the Sonnets remains unsurpassed.
ISBN 1-871551-38-2; A5 size; 200pp

## PHILOSOPHY

**Deals and Ideals** *by James Daly*

Alasdair MacIntyre writes of this book: "In his excellent earlier book *Marx: Justice and Dialectic* James Daly identified Marx's place in and extraordinary contribution to the moral debates of the modern era. Now he has put us even further in his debt not only by relating Marx to his Aristotelian predecessors and to the natural law tradition, but also by using this understanding of Marx to throw fresh light on the moral antagonism between Marx and individualist conceptions of human nature. This is a splendid sequel to his earlier work."

ISBN 1-87155-31-5; A5 size; 160pp

**Marx: Justice and Dialectic** *by James Daly*

Department of Scholastic Philosophy, Queen's University, Belfast.
James Daly shows the humane basis of Marx's thinking, rather than the imposed 'economic materialistic' views of many modem commentators. In particular he refutes the notion that for Marx, justice relates simply to the state of development of society at a particular time. Marx's views about justice and human relationships belong to the continuing traditions of moral thought in Europe.

ISBN 1-871551-28-5; A5 size; 180pp

**The Philosophy of Whitehead** *by T. E. Burke*

Department of Philosophy, University of Reading.
Dr Burke explores the main achievements of this philosopher, better known in the US than Britain. Whitehead, often remembered as Russell's tutor and collaborator on *Principia Mathematica,* was one of the few who had a grasp of relativity and its possible implications. His philosophical writings reflect his profound knowledge of mathematics and science. He was responsible for initiating process theology.

ISBN 1-871551-29-3; A5 size; 106pp

**Questions of Platonism** *by Ian Leask*

In a daring challenge to contemporary orthodoxy, Ian Leask subverts both Hegel and Heidegger by arguing for a radical re-evaluation of Platonism. Thus, while he traces a profoundly Platonic continuity between ancient Athens and 19th century Germany, the nature of this Platonism, he suggests, is neither 'totalizing' nor Hegelian but, instead, open-ended 'incomplete' and oriented towards a divine goal beyond *logos* or any metaphysical structure. Such a re-evaluation exposes the deep anti-Platonism of Hegel's absolutizing of volitional subjectivity; it also confirms Schelling as true modern heir to the 'constitutive incompletion' of Plato and Plotinus. By providing a more nuanced approach - refusing to accept either Hegel's self-serving account of 'Platonism' or the (equally totalizing) post-Heideggerian inversion of this narrative – Leask demonstrates the continued relevance of a genuine, 'finite' Platonic quest. Ian Leask teaches in the Department of Scholastic Philosophy at the Queen's University of Belfast.

ISBN 1-871551-32-3; A5 size; 154pp

## FICTION

**The Case of the Scarlet Woman – Sherlock Holmes and the Occult**

*by Watkin Jones*

A haunted house, a mysterious kidnapping and a poet's demonic visions are just the beginnings of three connected cases that lead Sherlock Holmes into confrontation with the infamous black magician Aleister Crowley and, more sinisterly, his scorned Scarlet Woman.

The fact that Dr Watson did not publish details of these investigations is perhaps testament to the unspoken fear he and Holmes harboured for the supernatural. *The Case of the Scarlet Woman* convinced them both that some things cannot be explained by cold logic.

ISBN 1-871551-14-5; A5 size; 130pp

## THEATRE

**Music Hall Warriors: A history of the Variety Artistes Federation**

*by Peter Honri*

This is an unique and fascinating history of how vaudeville artistes formed the first effective actor's trade union in 1906 and then battled with the powerful owners of music halls to obtain fairer contracts. The story continues with the VAF dealing with performing rights, radio, and the advent of television. Peter Honri is the fourth generation of a vaudeville family. The book has a foreword by the Right Honourable John Major MP when he was Prime Minister – his father was a founder member of the VAF.

ISBN 1-871551-06-4; A4 size; 140pp; illus.